RVing America's Backroads:

Robert Longsdorf, Jr.

. . . Light-hearted I take to the open road,
Healthy, free, the world before me,
The long brown path before me leading
wherever I choose."

Walt Whitman, *Song of the Open Road*

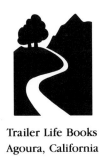

Trailer Life Books
Agoura, California

DEDICATION

For Donna: Rough and smooth
we've traveled the roads together.

Trailer Life Book Division

President: Richard Rouse
Vice President/General Manager: Ted Binder
Vice President/Publisher, Book Division: Michael Schneider
General Manager, Book Division: Rena Copperman
Assistant Manager, Book Division: Cindy Lang

Cover design: Bob Schroeder
Cover photograph: Robert Longsdorf, Jr.
Interior design: David Fuller/Robert S. Tinnon
Production manager: Rena Copperman
Editorial assistant: Judi Lazarus
Indexer: Barbara Wurf
Maps: EarthSurface Graphics

All photographs are the author's unless otherwise credited.

This book was set in ITC Garamond Book by Publisher's
Typography and printed on 60-pound Consoweb Brilliant by
R.R. Donnelley and Sons in Willard, Ohio.

ISBN 0-934798-11-7

Library of Congress Cataloging-in-Publication Data

Longsdorf, Robert, 1941–
    RVing America's backroads: California.

    Includes index.
    1. Automobiles—California—Touring. 2. Recreational
vehicles—California. 3. California—Description
and travel—1981–   —Guide-books. I. Title.
GV1024.L57 1989   917.94   86-50522
ISBN 0–934798–11–7

Contents

OTHER BOOKS BY TRAILER LIFE

An RVer's Annual: The Best of Trailer Life and MotorHome
Edited by Rena Copperman

This collector's edition of the best travel, technical, personality, and feature articles from past issues of the magazines, acknowledged as the leading publications in the RV field, is topped off with a special "Constitution" feature, recalling the recent nationwide anniversary celebration in prose and pictures. Beautiful four-color photos throughout . . . a great gift idea.
8½ × 11, 208 pages
$15.95 ISBN: 0-934798-21-4

Full-time RVing: A Complete Guide to Life on the Open Road
Bill and Jan Moeller

The answers to all the questions anyone who dreams of traveling full time in an RV may have can be found in this remarkable new source book. *Full-time RVing* takes the mystery out of fulltiming and makes it possible to fully enjoy this once-in-a-lifetime experience.
7¼ × 9¼, 352 pages
$14.95 ISBN: 0-934798-14-1

RX for RV Performance & Mileage
John Geraghty and Bill Estes

In 32 chapters, this book covers everything an owner must know about how an engine (particularly a V-8) works, vehicle maintenance, propane and diesel as alternative fuels, eliminating engine "ping," improving exhaust systems and fuel economy, and much more.
7¾ × 9¼, 359 pages
$14.95 ISBN: 0-934798-08-0

The Good Sam RV Cookbook
Edited by Beverly Edwards and the editors of *Trailer Life*

Over 250 easy and delicious recipes, including 78 prize-winners from Good Sam Samboree cook-offs around the country. Also contains tips, ideas, and suggestions to help you get the most from your RV galley.
7¼ × 9¼, 252 pages
$14.95 ISBN: 0-934798-17-6

These books are available at fine bookstores everywhere. Or, you may order directly from Trailer Life. For each book ordered, simply send us the name of the book, the price, plus $2 per book for shipping and handling (California residents please add 6½% sales tax). Mail to:

Trailer Life Books, P.O. Box 4500, Agoura, CA 91301

You may call our Customer Service representatives if you wish to charge your order or if you want more information. Please phone, toll-free, Monday through Friday, 7:00 A.M. to 6:00 P.M.; Saturday, 7:30 A.M. to 12:30 P.M. Pacific Time, **1-800-234-3450.**

Preface

Y ou have before you the first volume in an exciting new series of books written specifically for RVers; books that address the unique interests and needs of those who know the special joy of travel by trailer or motorhome.

This backroads series has been several years in the writing, requiring thousands of miles of driving and months of research for each volume. By actually traveling the routes outlined in each of these books the authors have been able to capture the essence of each region. Within these pages are captured the sights, sounds, and aromas of the various corners of America — those fascinating locales that lie along the roads less traveled.

While the theme here is backroading, you will note that some of the routes outlined take in a few familiar destinations. That is not as paradoxical as it appears, because we have found that even the well-traveled offers the unexplored. For example, the small side streets of San Francisco's Chinatown offer treasures for those who take the time to venture from the crowds on Grant Avenue. And, in the famed Napa Valley wine country, we hope you'll take time to explore some of the small wineries often overlooked by tourists. On the other hand, we have deliberately avoided destinations such as Yosemite National Park, which is undeniably beautiful but so overcrowded that, for most of the year, it has the pace and atmosphere of a major metropolitan area.

As comprehensive as these books are, however, bear in mind that they are meant to be a guide, an introduction to the areas outlined in each suggested tour. In short, we are going to get you there, but we hope you will maximize the enjoyment of your travels by taking advantage of local resources for additional information on the respective areas.

During the summer months, for instance, reservations may be advisable at certain attractions, and a call in advance may save hours of frustration in waiting, or prevent the disappointment of being turned away. It's especially important to note that many attractions offer discounts that may be best arranged for by calling ahead. An example is the Golden Eagle Passport offered by the federal government. It presently costs $25 a year and can be obtained in person or by mail from the National Park Service, U.S. Department of the Interior, 18th and C streets, N.W., Washington, D.C. 20240. The Golden Age Passport is free to permanent U.S. residents who are 62 or older; the Golden Access Passport is free to permanently blind or disabled travelers. These latter two must be applied for in person at most federally operated recreation areas that charge an entrance fee.

Finally, bear in mind that while every attempt has been made to assure that information on routes, road conditions, entrance fees and other factual matter was accurate at press time, inevitably things change. Therefore, as you retrace my route and follow in my footsteps I urge you to draw upon these same sources to supplement this guide.

I hope that this book will be of value in your travels and that its pages will provide you with the same sensations of discovery and joy that I found in the research and writing.

ACKNOWLEDGMENTS

The Publisher wishes to thank the following people for their valuable assistance in furnishing time, material, and support in the production of this book:

Michele Burgess, Lori Nelson and the California Office of Tourism, Doug Emerson, George Ostertag, Riverside County's National Date Festival, Napa Chamber of Commerce, John Thompson of Trees of Mystery, Joseph Woods, Tom Le Rose, Finley Holiday Films, FVN Corporation, Bureau of Reclamation, Nevada City Chamber of Commerce, Jim Elder, Charles Moore, Tuolomne County Visitors' Bureau, Bob Howells, and all the helpful people in these organizations who were so prompt and willing to help.

Those colleagues of ours who deserve special thanks are Judi Lazarus (for wise and witty consul), Gale Urtel (for overseeing details of typesetting), Bob Tinnon (for his curmudgeonly assistance on innumerable matters of design and production), Mirante Almazan (for expert advice on color), Alice Ackerly, Mary Andert, Toni LeGras, and all the other people too numerous to mention by name that have contributed to this book.

Quotation on page 72 © by Hunter S. Thompson. Reprinted with permission of Summit Books, a division of Simon & Schuster, Inc.

CALIFORNIA

Joseph Woods

Beginning with early Spanish exploration, through the gold rush and into the present, California has achieved an almost mythical status as a land of vast potential. It is that promise that has drawn millions of travelers to the Golden State.

Lately, though, the luster has been dulled somewhat by reports of smog, earthquakes, mudslides, and traffic jams that have eclipsed the images of snow-capped mountains, sandy beaches, and Pacific sunsets. The people of California have also become a target of the bemused observations of social satirists who often characterize them as being trendy, eager to embrace the latest in fad and fashion and, collectively, a bit too laid back and just slightly off-center.

But in truth California remains a place of nearly unlimited promise. Boasting a coastline that combines the sandy beaches of the south with the rugged beauty of the north, the tallest point—Mount Whitney at 14,494 feet—and the lowest point—Death Valley at 282 feet below sea level—in the lower forty eight states, California is a land of unparalleled diversity. At certain times of the year it is literally possible to cool off with a dip in the Pacific in the morning, and hit the ski slopes in the afternoon.

As for the people, it's important to note that California is a wonderful melting pot. When the Spaniards arrived, they found a relatively large number of Indians of diversified tongues and cultures already in existence. Add to that the later influx of Southerners, Easterners, Northerners, and Midwesterners, as well as people from more distant lands who have come together and you have a cultural bouillabaisse that greatly enhances the state's already extensive riches. True, travelers may encounter the odd and the eccentric, but they'll also be greeted by some of the most hospitable people to be found anywhere.

No wonder, then, that California has long been a popular destination for RVers. From the snowbirds who flock to the state in the winter to bask in the therapeutic climate of the high desert country of Southern California, to vacationers who travel the length and breadth of the state throughout the year, sampling its amusements and scenic wonders, California has an almost irresistible allure.

Much of that allure comes from those things to be found off the beaten path. It is the forty-niners who are credited with the state's motto, Eureka—"I have found it." I hope these tours prompt you to say at the end of your travels—Eureka!

Jim Elder

George Ostertag

The North Coast Redwoods

Moist, cool and green; and shade the violets,
That they may bind the moss in leafy nets.
A filbert hedge with wild briar overtwined,
And clumps of woodbine taking the soft wind
Upon their summer thrones; there too
should be
The frequent chequer of a youngling tree,
That with a score of light green bretheren
shoots
From the quaint mossiness of aged roots. . . .

John Keats, "I Stood Tiptoe"

I n a state blessed with an embarrassment of riches, the majestic coast redwoods — *Sequoia sempervirens* — have to be counted as one of California's most magnificent treasures. Limited to a 450-mile range that extends from Big Sur to the Oregon–California line, these awesome giants, the oldest living trees on earth, can be viewed at a number of preserves throughout their shrinking domain. From the small groves of Big Sur State Park and Muir Woods, near San Francisco, to the 106,000-acre Redwoods National Park just south of the coastal community of Crescent City, travelers are provided with a number of opportunities to stroll mossy, sun-splashed paths, get close to the redwoods, and experience their overwhelming majesty.

The Redwood Empire Route

Having had a chance to explore the full length of the redwood range, some of my fondest recollections are of the approximately 150-mile US 101 route from Richardson Grove State Park to magnificent Redwoods National Park. Here, along the route dubbed the Redwood Highway, there is an opportunity to see some of the finest specimens of the coast redwoods, explore an almost limitless network of backroads, take in some largely unseen coastal vistas, visit the picturesque Victorian town of Ferndale or walk the historic sites of Eureka, the largest community on California's North Coast.

Anyone visiting the Redwood Empire region, the heart of the redwood country, will quickly discover that it has two distinct identities. Except for a few miles, from the hamlet of Piercy to Eureka, the highway lies mainly inland, cutting a wide swath between the giant trees. North of Eureka and Arcata the highway narrows to two lanes of rolling and winding road that is often darkened by the shade of the dense stands of redwoods as it parallels the Pacific coastline.

Richardson Grove: A Closeup of the Redwoods

Since I was driving a motorhome that exceeded the thirty-foot limit in the nearby state park facilities, I began my exploration below Eureka by setting up camp at Benbow Valley RV Resort, just south of the town of Garberville. From Benbow it was easy to backtrack the six miles to the entrance to Richardson Grove State Park where I had an opportunity to stroll among the trees along shaded, winding trails and get my first close-up look at this region's towering redwoods.

Richardson Grove, named for a former California governor, represents one of the first successful efforts of the Save-the-Redwoods League to acquire and protect the venerable coast redwoods. The conservation group, which has raised millions of dollars for redwood preservation since its founding in 1919, persuaded the state to purchase the initial 120

Tour 1 160 miles
Side trip to Ferndale, 7 miles

RICHARDSON GROVE STATE PARK •
BENBOW LAKE STATE
RECREATION AREA • EEL RIVER •
GARBERVILLE • SHELTER COVE •
HUMBOLDT REDWOODS STATE
PARK • FERNDALE • CENTERVILLE
BEACH COUNTY PARK • EUREKA •
FORT HUMBOLDT • SEQUOIA PARK •
TRINIDAD STATE BEACH • DRY
LAGOON • REDWOOD NATIONAL
PARK • PRAIRIE CREEK STATE PARK •
DEL NORTE COAST STATE PARK •
JEDEDIAH SMITH REDWOODS
STATE PARK • KLAMATH RIVER •
CRESCENT CITY

North Coast Backroads.
Dotted with state parks and beaches and a seemingly limitless number of narrow, tree-shaded side roads, the North Coast is the quintessence of backroad RVing.

Foggy Beauty.
The ubiquitous coastal fog enhances the
stunning beauty of the redwood groves
at Prairie Creek Redwoods State Park.

Loerner Krytein

acres that make up the heart of this park in 1922. Further acreage was
added throughout the 1920s, and land acquisition over subsequent years
has now brought the total park land to 1,000 acres.

I found this park especially appealing because, despite its respectable
size, it is still much smaller than most of the other parks in the Redwood
Highway chain. That gives the visitor an intimate atmosphere that
enhances the pleasure of strolling the many easy trails. Of particular

interest is the self-guided Redwood Trail featuring a number of exhibits, including a fallen tree illustrating the unique adaptive ability that allows these giants to survive the many natural catastrophes that time and the elements hurl at them.

Except for the height of the tourist season during midsummer, when, according to park rangers, Richardson Grove becomes especially popular with travelers, you can find an abundance of RV parking on the small bluff that overlooks the Eel River. You'll also be delighted to learn that the park boasts 170 campsites in its Huckleberry and Oak Flat campgrounds. Located across the river, the Oak Flat facility is closed in the fall when the access bridge is removed to prepare for the Eel's higher water level. A fifteen-day-stay limit is enforced year-round, and RV camping is limited to trailers under twenty-four feet and motorhomes under thirty feet long.

After a stopover at Richardson Grove, you can begin your tour of the redwood country in earnest by turning north out of the park entrance. Shortly after you pass one of the ubiquitous redwood-souvenir stands on the right (you'll be surprised by the number of items that can be made from redwood and redwood burls), US 101 bursts from the shade of the giant trees and widens into the four-lane interstate.

Benbow Lake Area

Within a few miles of rejoining the interstate, I recommend that you take the time to stop, if only briefly, at the Benbow Lake State Recreation Area, located on the west side of the highway at the Benbow turnoff. This facility (which is only a lake in the summer when the Eel River is temporarily impounded by the Benbow Dam) is especially inviting, and I paused long enough for lunch in the grassy picnic area. Although the lake was not filled during my early March visit, the folks at the Benbow campground told me they recommended it highly to summer visitors. Because powerboating and water skiing are prohibited, serenity reigns most of the time, with sunbathers lining the lakeshore and kayaks and canoes lazily skimming the lake's glassy surface. But, as with a few of the other areas in this lower section of redwood country, I was also told that Benbow Lake attracts a fair number of summertime visitors who flock to its cool waters to find a respite from the 90° temperatures that are not uncommon here during the months of July and August.

Reformed Garberville

Just three miles farther north from the lake there is another turnoff to the forgettable town of Garberville. With a population of a little more than 1,000, Garberville was founded on timber and is still largely supported by the logging operations that are becoming uncomfortably more prevalent throughout this region. In recent years Garberville had also gained considerable notoriety as the unofficial capital of the Humboldt County marijuana industry. Many stores in town openly sold equipment, supplies, and how-to literature for growers, and the local paper carried a

Redwood Souvenirs.
From stoic Indian chiefs to intricate totems, visitors to California's North Coast will find a variety of artifacts fashioned from fallen redwoods.

regular feature, "The Bust Barometer," charting the recent raids of the illegal pot fields.

Happily much of that activity is a thing of the past (it's hard to say that it has been totally stamped out), thanks to a series of raids by state and federal law enforcement officals. Now, Garberville at least has the appearance of a law-abiding community, but still maintains a vaguely unfriendly frontier atmosphere. In short, there is little to recommend it as a tourist stop. About the only reason to exit the interstate here is to get fuel for your rig or pick up groceries. Before dismissing it altogether, however, I should also add that there are some early signs that Garberville may be recognizing the fact that it is sitting on a gold mine of possibilities as a strategically located tourist center. I spotted a couple of craft shops; there may be more such establishments by now.

Perhaps one other reason for exiting at Garberville is to pick up the Thorne/Shelter Cove Road that heads west to the coast and the hamlet of Shelter Cove. I was advised not to take the road because my rig was too big for the sharp turns — although one resident told me it would be all right if I took it slowly — so I didn't get a chance to explore the route firsthand.

For the stalwart who might want to give it a try, here's what information I was able to gather: Open year-round, the road covers twenty-three narrow, steep, winding miles before reaching the planned retirement community of Shelter Cove. A private campground with hookups is located at the cove, and the small boat harbor purportedly has some sportfishing boats available for charter. Fishing is said to be excellent.

Driving the Redwood Highway

Continuing north from Garberville, US 101 offers a turnout where a map of the Redwood Highway and its many side roads has been etched into a wooden sign. The sign directs travelers to the turnoff that leads to the spectacular scenic thirty-three-mile drive known as the Avenue of the Giants. It also notes towns and special points of interest.

Along a route that roughly parallels the south fork of the Eel River, you'll wind through dark and damp redwood groves; past the small communities of Phillipsville, Miranda, Myers Flat, Weott, and Pepperwood; and encounter special attractions including the One Log House and Chimney Tree (both near Phillipsville), the Drive Thru Tree (not big enough for RVs), the Immortal Tree, the Eternal Tree House, and, of course, a host of redwood-souvenir shops.

The 47,000-acre Humboldt Redwoods State Park is also included in this route; it's worth taking some extra time to explore since it contains some of the finest old-growth trees in the Redwood Empire. Turnouts are well marked — although they are sometimes a bit cramped for RVs — and signs at each of these will direct you to the memorial groves that honor noteworthy individuals. Along this route you'll also find a number of campgrounds, both public and private. **Note:** The state facilities all limit RVs to those under thirty feet.

Traveler's Guide.
North of Garberville take time to get your bearings by stopping at the etched sign that guides travelers through the Redwood Highway.

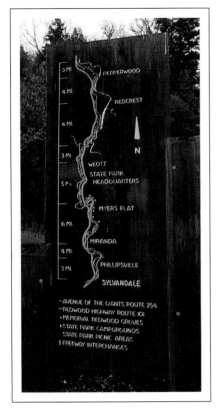

©FVN Corp.

Redwood Highway.
The Redwood Highway winds through dappled groves of towering trees as it loops around some of the most scenic spots on the North Coast.

North of Weott, Mattole Road extends westward into Humboldt Redwoods State Park, eventually winding into and up over the small mountain range that separates the Redwood Empire Valley from the coast. Detailed maps of the region indicate that this road leads all the way to the little town of Petrolia and Cape Mendocino — the most westerly point in the continental United States — before it loops back around through the towns of Ferndale and Loleta and rejoins US 101. I followed this road for a time, with the intention of completing the entire loop. Unfortunately I ran into rain and heavy fog and, limited by the size of my rig, I wasn't able to explore the entire route. The small section I did drive appeared to be in good shape and fairly easy to navigate. I could find no warnings in any of the local tourist information to indicate that the road was not passable for RVs; however, I would advise checking in Weott or with one of the state park rangers to get accurate information on road conditions.

Speaking of weather, it's important to point out here that as you travel north and get closer to the coast the weather becomes more fickle. While the Eel River Valley is usually bathed in sunshine and, as noted earlier, often hot in the summer, from Eureka on, as US 101 moves closer to the coast, you're likely to encounter (at worst), low, dense fog and intermittent and sometimes furious ocean-borne rain squalls or, at best, a pervasive, gray overcast that hangs heavily over the landscape. A resident of the North Coast told me that as a rule of thumb, if the sun is going to shine the overcast will burn off by 10 A.M.; if it's not gone by then, it's a safe bet that you won't see the sun all day.

The coast redwood is the world's tallest tree, with mature trees averaging between 200 to 250 feet in height, and 10 to 15 feet in diameter. These redwoods have an average life span of 400 to 800 years; however, individual trees have been dated at more than 2,000 years old. The redwoods grow from both cone seeds and sprouts generated on injured or fallen trees. Mature trees generally produce seeds every year, which are of almost microscopic size. It can take as many as 120,000 seeds to weigh just one pound.

Historic Ferndale.
From elaborate and colorful homes (*upper left*), to the quaint cottage, "Ferndale," built by pioneer Seth Shaw in 1854 (*upper right*), the picturesque community of Ferndale is a feast for lovers of Victoriana. Built in 1875, the Arnold Berding home (*lower left*) is only one of many Ferndale structures now listed on the National Register of Historic Places.

Ferndale — A Walk through the Past

Whether you reach Ferndale through its back door, via Mattole Road, or by US 101, taking the well-marked turnoff about ten miles south of Eureka and crossing the seventy-five-year-old arched Fernbridge, be sure to save some time in your itinerary to explore this quaint Victorian village. Ferndale was settled in 1852 by Vermonters Seth and Stephen Shaw, but it was Danish pioneers who established the town's dairy industry in the 1850s. The whole town has been designated a state historic landmark and, given that distinction, it's easy to see why Ferndale residents are fired with a fierce civic pride that has inspired an ongoing restoration program aimed at reviving the town's many historic structures.

Your best bet for getting details of the town's early days is to stop by the museum at Third and Shaw streets and pick up an informative brochure that provides directions for a suggested walking tour of the town. Some words of warning: RV parking is nonexistent on Main Street, and limited on some of the side streets. Arriving as I did on a Wednesday in early spring, I had no problem finding a parking spot just off Main on Shaw, near the museum. Had it been summer I am sure I wouldn't have been nearly so lucky.

I began my walking tour up Main, a fascinating street lined with freshly painted Victorian storefronts bearing whimsical names such as Tuzzy Muzzy, Withywindle, and Gepetto's. For me the highlight here is the Golden Gait Mercantile, an old-fashioned general store that takes you back to the turn of the century. The shelves of this store are jammed with bolts of cloth, patent medicines, old tins, and a host of simple and useful household items that you thought had gone the way of the horse

©FVN Corp.

and buggy. Youngsters will be delighted with the selection of wooden cars and tractors, kazoos, harmonicas, and the old-fashioned candy counter that features licorice whips, buttons, and jars of jaw breakers, jelly beans, and spice drops. All in all the store is a rare treat, and I found it hard to tear myself away.

After a stop for lunch at Roman's (Mexican-American fare), I walked back down Main to Shaw and east to Berding for a closer look at some of the restored homes. Without a doubt the most outstanding example of restoration is the Gingerbread Mansion, now a bed and breakfast inn on the corner of Berding and Brown streets. Decked out in bright yellow with orange trim, and guarded by stone dogs, this historic house was originally a hospital. It is meticulously landscaped and well deserving of its reputation as Ferndale's centerpiece of Victorian restoration.

Next door to the Gingerbread Mansion stands a much smaller and less lavishly trimmed house, painted an unusual red with white trim and proudly displaying a sign "Built in 1868." Another historic structure, the Arnold Berding Home, built in 1875, stands about a block off Main on Washington Street. The Shaw House, built in 1854 and named for Louis Shaw, is located on a large, shaded lot on Main. In addition to these few noteworthy examples, a number of less lavish but well-restored homes can be found on just about every street in town if you take the time to look for them.

Despite a dearth of parking, RVers will be happy to know Ferndale is a hospitable community that welcomes them by setting aside the nearby fairgrounds as a campground. The fairgrounds, located at the north edge of town on Van Ness Avenue, is open to RVers year-round, except during the county fair activities in August.

Victoriana.
The ornately decorated Gingerbread Mansion *(upper left)* has undergone extensive restoration, as have many private and commercial buildings throughout Ferndale.

Eureka's Sentinel.
The centerpiece of Eureka's Victorian heritage, the magnificent Carson Mansion, now a private club, stands majestically on a bluff overlooking the Pacific and historic Old Town.

Old Town Eateries.
A wide variety of dining experiences can be found within the restored restaurants of Old Town.

If you entered Ferndale from the main highway, before leaving the area you might want to take the time to drive out Centerville Road to Centerville Beach County Park. This four-acre park offers picnic tables and an opportunity to hike the beach and gather driftwood. Overnight camping is allowed for self-contained rigs; there are no hookups.

Eureka! We Have Found It

Back on US 101, it's a short ten miles north to Eureka, a town that one travel guide describes as a "good place to buy sewer pipe, lumber, a slab of redwood burl, a life-sized statue of a lumberjack carved from a redwood log, or a fresh fish dinner." The fact is that Eureka (population 24,000), despite its location, offers none of the quaint seaside ambiance one might expect to find in a North Coast community. However, a few attractions make a day's stay here worthwhile.

First, there is the Carson Mansion, a magnificent Victorian home built around 1885 that looms grandly at the north end of 2nd Street near Eureka's Old Town section. This pale-green structure accented with dark-green trim has become a symbol of Eureka's Victorian past. Unfortunately, it is a private men's club, not open to the public.

Back down 2nd Street lies Old Town, an area of restored Victorian storefronts that now house arts and crafts shops, antique stores, and several restaurants. A red brick street runs the length of this historic section and in the summer rings with the clip-clop of a horse-drawn carriage that carries visitors up and down the street. RVers will find ample parking in several nearby lots. Besides being located within easy walking distance of Old Town, these parking areas are also handy to the Humboldt Bay waterfront. For a special treat take the bay tour on the MV *Madaket* across to Samoa peninsula, and sit down to a sumptuous lunch at the Samoa Cookhouse.

One nearby attraction (just off 2nd Street, at 3rd and E streets) is the Clarke Memorial Museum, which contains a number of exhibits relating to local and regional history. The comprehensive collection of Indian baskets and artifacts is exceptional.

Historic Humboldt

Backtracking a few miles to Eureka's southern outskirts, I recommend a stop at Fort Humboldt, a California State Historical Park that sits high atop a bluff overlooking Humboldt Bay. Established in 1853 under the command of Lieutenant Colonel Robert C. Buchanan, the post was assigned the task of maintaining peace in the area and protecting Eureka's early settlers. Interestingly enough, one of the soldiers assigned to the fort shortly after its founding was a young lieutenant named Ulysses S. Grant. After serving for four months, Grant wrote his family that he found the post so lonely and inhospitable that he was quitting the Army and coming home. When he left Eureka in 1854 he told those he left behind: "Whoever hears of me in ten years will hear of a well-to-do Missouri farmer."

Within the last three years Fort Humboldt has undergone extensive renovation and, though construction was still going on at the time of my visit, many of the buildings have been returned to their original form. The entire fort complex now contains nearly twenty structures, ranging from the commanding officer's quarters, troop quarters, and hospital, to the stables, magazine, and an old bake house. A bonus for visitors to this area is the fascinating outdoor logging display, located on the grounds at the north end of the fort compound. This display traces the history of North Coast logging from its beginnings in the 1850s to the present. There is a self-guided trail, accessible to the handicapped, and exhibits include an authentic logger's cabin, a variety of tools, and an 1882 "steam donkey" (the replacement for the ox teams that up to then had been used to haul logs). Admission to both the fort and the logging exhibits is free.

Before leaving Eureka, travelers might want to make one more stop at the beautiful Sequoia Park (off Harris Street on W Street), where fern-lined trails wind through a fifty-four-acre stand of virgin redwoods. For the youngsters, this park also houses the Sequoia Zoo, complete with duck pond, petting zoo, flower garden and playground.

The North Coast Redwoods

Shortly after rounding the bend from downtown Eureka, US 101 crosses the bridge over Eureka Slough, loops around Arcata Bay, and then straightens out into a wide-open northward route heading to Arcata and the magnificent redwood groves of the North Coast.

Fort Exhibits.
Fort Humboldt combines exhibits on the region's early military history with a wide variety of equipment and artifacts that commemorate the logging operations of the North Coast.

State Park Vista.
Huge rock formations, wind-gnarled trees, picnic grounds, and superb coastal vistas await travelers who take the time to explore the backroads of Patrick's Point State Park.

Arcata, which is the home of Humboldt State University, also has a good selection of restored Victorian homes scattered throughout the town. A map listing these homes can be obtained from the chamber of commerce office located downtown on G Street. During your stop in Arcata you might also want to stop by Jocoby's Storehouse, a restored 1857 packtrain warehouse that has been converted into a shopping center, housing craft and antique shops and restaurants.

From Arcata north, US 101 becomes a more narrow corridor hemmed in by lush greenery and towering redwoods. Any number of exits along this stretch will offer access to the coast. Despite the fact that the coast was heavily overcast on the morning I hit this stretch of 101, I took a chance and exited at Trinidad State Beach (the exit is well marked). For my efforts I was rewarded with an absolutely breathtaking view of the rugged coastline.

After parking the motorhome in the large parking area at the end of the Trinidad road, a few steps to the edge of the bluff overlooking the ocean gave me a magnificent view through the trees to the coastline below. I stood watching the Pacific swells gather offshore and break against a large tree-topped island before washing onto the rocky beach.

It's a marvelous scene, even under leaden skies, and I urge travelers to make a stop here if only for the few brief minutes it takes to capture it on film. If you have more time to spend, pack a picnic lunch and walk down the steep path to the beach.

Just north of the Trinidad State Beach turnoff, US 101 narrows abruptly to two lanes as it dips and winds up the coast, following the uneven contours of the rugged coastline. Along this stretch of highway you'll find numerous backroad possibilities that turn west to state beaches and other coastal recreation areas, or east into the dim shadows of the redwood groves. On an impulse I took one of those turns onto an unmarked dirt road and found myself on a deserted logging road, winding among towering redwoods and a forest floor lushly carpeted with huge ferns. During the fall, winter, and early spring when timber operations are not in full swing, such side trips are possible; from about May to September when logging trucks are plying those routes, I would advise sticking to the roads marked on your map.

Among the numerous areas ripe for exploration here, there are stops known respectively as Big Lagoon, Freshwater Lagoon, and Dry Lagoon. I was touched by the forbidding beauty of the windswept and eerily desolate Dry Lagoon. Besides offering easy access to a wide, sandy beach, huge hunks of driftwood are scattered along the coast as far as the eye can see. It's a truly remarkable sight.

Touring Redwood National Park

North of these lagoons US 101 turns slightly inland before reaching the entrance to the southern arm of Redwood National Park just north of the town of Orick. As luck would have it, before proceeding on to the park I decided to stop on the outskirts of Orick for lunch at the Park Café. Housed in a rather nondescript building next to a motel, the café serves food that rivals a lot of big-city restaurants. In fact, the waitress served me one of the best — and biggest — bowls of New England clam chowder I have ever had. How big was it? Well, by the time I finished the chowder I had to ask the waitress to pack the sandwich I had also ordered to go. If you can't make it for lunch, try stopping for dinner when you can choose from a menu that offers such unique fare as elk steak in wild mushroom sauce, buffalo steak, wild boar roast, Wiener schnitzel, or calamari in lemon butter.

The best way to begin a tour of Redwood National Park is to stop first at the information center south of Orick and pick up one of the free brochures offered by the National Park Service. That brochure will serve as a good, but very basic, guide to the five separate areas that make up the park. For more detailed information you might want to choose a book from the wide selection that is available for purchase.

Although Redwood National Park was not officially established until 1968, its origins could be said to date back more than fifty years to when the Save-the-Redwoods League began its active campaign to preserve and protect old-growth forests. Alarmed by a steady increase in logging

Finley-Holiday Films

Logging Miles.
Logging trucks travel through some of the spectacular, pristine areas of Redwood National Park. RVers should keep a wary eye out for the large trucks.

Finley-Holiday Films

Touring the Redwoods.
RVers who take the time to get off the beaten path and explore the numerous side roads of the region will be rewarded with unsurpassed views of the giant redwoods.

that by 1947 was taking one million board feet of lumber per year from the redwood groves, the league petitioned the state legislature and the federal government to pass legislation that would set aside a certain portion of the redwoods for preservation. Finally, when a 1960 study showed that only 300,000 acres remained out of an original two million acres of redwoods, President Lyndon B. Johnson signed the act in 1968 establishing the basic park boundaries that encompassed some 50,000 acres. In 1978, after further studies indicated that continued logging operations were destroying valuable watershed, President Jimmy Carter signed a law that brought another 48,000 acres of redwoods into the park. Today the park, which includes three state parks — Prairie Creek, Del Norte Coast, and Jedediah Smith — spans a total of more than 109,000 acres.

Just north of Orick, a right turn puts you on Bald Hills Road, which leads to Lady Bird Johnson Grove and the Tall Trees Grove clustered along the banks of Redwood Creek. In the summertime, shuttle bus service is offered between the Redwood Information Center and these groves. RVers might want to take advantage of this service since much of the Bald Hills route is off-limits to trailers and larger RVs. For trailer owners who want to use their own transportation, the Park Service provides a temporary trailer-storage lot at the Redwood Creek Trailhead and Information Center. If you want to view the world's tallest tree, the shuttle bus will drop you at the Redwood Creek Trailhead; from there it's an 8.5-mile hike back to Tall Trees Grove and the giant tree that rises 367.8 feet from the forest floor. Allow a total of about eight hours hiking time for the walk to and from the tree.

Back on US 101, a few miles up the highway, just before the county fish hatchery, Davison Road turns to the left and winds down to the coast into Prairie Creek State Park. This is a narrow, gravel road that park rangers told me was not suited to large motorhomes, and trailers are positively forbidden. If you can find some way of making the trip, you'll be rewarded by a spectacular view of the coast and a chance to view the wild elk herds that graze here in the summer.

For those who can't make it into Prairie Creek this way, the main entrance to the park can be found a few miles farther north off the main highway. Stop here, if only to take time to browse through the excellent natural history museum located in the information center. There are also good hiking trails leading in several directions from the parking lot, as well as a very scenic campground nestled in the redwoods. A special path, the Revelation Trail, contains interpretive signs in Braille and is wheelchair accessible. At the time of my visit a herd of Roosevelt elk, just starting to shed their winter coats, were browsing in the pastureland near the visitor center.

From the Prairie Creek Park entrance, US 101 continues north, sliding deeper into the shadows of the thick redwoods, passing a number of memorial groves. Several miles north of the park entrance, look for a sign on the left that marks the start of the Coastal Drive. Partially paved and

Browsing Elk.
Shedding their winter coats, Roosevelt elk browse peacefully among the redwoods and the open coastal areas in Prairie Creek Redwoods State Park.

partially gravel, the road is passable for both motorhomes and trailers from the highway to Alder Camp Road. Take the time to pause and enjoy the beach.

Taking Alder Camp Road will lead you back out to US 101 where, after rounding a curve and taking the bridge over the magificent Klamath River, you'll come to Requa Road, another left turnoff that leads to a picnic area and the start of the Coastal Trail. This trail loops down to the coast and back up Lagoon Creek, covering a total of four miles one way. I did not get a chance to walk it, but the folks at park headquarters said it passes through some excellent beach area. Guided interpretive walks are offered in the summer.

Del Norte and Crescent City

From the Klamath area, a ten-mile drive north on US 101 will take you to the Del Norte Coast Redwoods State Park. Not, however, before you reach the popular tourist spot designated by the large sign proclaiming "Trees of Mystery." The folks at the souvenir shop claim that this is one of the most heavily visited attractions on the North Coast. Judging by the traffic in the parking lot, I believe it. Those who want to spring for the admission fee will have an opportunity to walk through a hollow tree into a private park that features many oddly shaped redwoods. It should also be noted that the parking lot features huge statues of Paul Bunyan and Babe the Blue Ox. Paul is wired for sound and offers greetings to those on their way to the gift shop.

Noted for its variety of wildlife and foliage, the more sedate 6,400-acre Del Norte State Park has as its most popular feature the 2.5-mile Damnation Creek Trail, which leads from a trailhead just off the main highway out to the coast. Mill Creek Campground is also located here, open from April 1 to October 31. From this park it is only a few more miles into

Mysteries of Nature.
Paul Bunyan and his blue ox, Babe, greet visitors who come to walk the nature trails and inspect the Trees of Mystery and the End of the Trail Museum near Del Norte Coast Redwoods State Park.

©FVN Corp.

15

Crescent City Lighthouse.
Tide permitting, guided tours are offered at this old working lighthouse-museum, where you can see the original light, antique clocks, and photos of shipwrecks.

©FVN Corp.

Looking Up into the Redwoods.
Sun filters through the lofty redwoods, inspiring serenity and awe.

©FVN Corp.

Crescent City; here you can stop at Redwood National Park Headquarters for further information and to learn more about the special interpretive programs offered throughout the summer months. In Crescent City itself, the Battery Point Lighthouse (at the end of A Street) is worth a stop, as is the Del Norte County Museum. At the museum you will find information on the disastrous shipwreck on July 30, 1865, of the *Brother Jonathan*. There are also details on a more recent calamity, a tidal wave that swept the coast here in the wake of the 1964 Alaska earthquake.

Jedediah Smith Redwoods State Park

North of Crescent City you can visit Jedediah Smith Redwoods State Park by taking the narrow US 199 cutoff from US 101. At the entrance to the park you have a choice of following the paved South Fork Road that follows the Smith River's south fork through the redwoods into Big Flat Campground. Another choice for adventurous backroaders is the paved Douglas Park Road that leads to the unpaved, narrow, winding Howland Hill Road. Once an old stagecoach road, this route has been widened some to permit passage of motorized vehicles. The Park Service rangers told me that trailers are not recommended here, but that small motorhomes may be appropriate. To be on the safe side, check at the park visitor center for road conditions.

Special points of interest in this park include the National Tribute Grove dedicated to the men and women who served in World Wars I and II. The park's largest redwood — 340 feet tall and 16 feet in diameter — can be found in Stout Grove.

POINTS OF INTEREST: California Tour 1

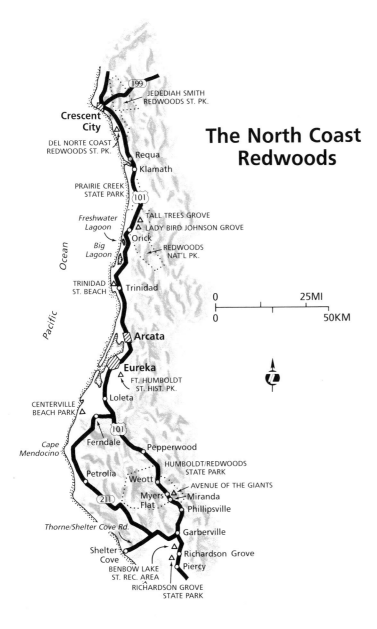

The North Coast Redwoods

RESTAURANTS:
Crescent City: *Harbor View Grotto,* on Citizen's Dock Road, (707) 464-3815; steaks and seafood.

Eureka: *Samoa Cookhouse,* across Samoa Bridge from Eureka, (707) 442-1659; American food served "lumber-camp style": *Eureka Seafood Grotto,* 6th and Broadway Streets, (707) 443-1673.

Ferndale: *Roman's,* on Main Street at north end of town, (707) 725-6358; Mexican-American; Sunday brunch.

Garberville: *Benbow Inn,* 445 Lake Benbow Drive, open mid-April-January 1, (707) 923-2124; Continental cuisine.

ANNUAL EVENTS:
Crescent City: *World Championship Crab Races,* February; *Seafood Festival,* September.

Eureka: *Live steam engine demonstrations,* Fort Humboldt State Historic Park, May-September.

Ferndale: *Christmas Gala,* Dec.

MUSEUMS AND GALLERIES:
Eureka: *Clarke Museum,* 3rd and E Streets, (707) 443-1947, year-round except New Year's Day, Easter, Memorial Day, Thanksgiving and Christmas. *Samoa Cookhouse Museum,* off US 101 across the Samoa Bridge, (707) 442-1659, year-round except Thanksgiving and Christmas.

Ferndale: *Ferndale Museum,* Third and Shaw streets, (707) 786-4466, irregular hours, inquire in town.

SPECIAL ATTRACTIONS:
Eureka: *Fort Humboldt State Historic Park,* 3431 Fort Ave. 95501, (707) 445-6567, year-round except major holidays. Four to five RV spaces. Call ahead.

Klamath: *Trees of Mystery and End of the Trail Museum,* on Redwood Highway, US 101, (707) 482-5613, call for hours.

ACCESS: *US 101* at Richardson Grove State Park, north to Jedediah Smith Redwoods State Park.

INFORMATION: *Redwood Empire Association,* One Market Plaza, Spear Street Tower, Suite 1001, San Francisco, California, 94105 (415) 543-8334; *Eureka Chamber of Commerce,* 2112 Broadway, Eureka, California 95501, (707) 442-3738, (800) 356-6381 in California; *Redwood National Park,* 1111 2nd Street, Crescent City, California 95531, (707) 464-6101. *Ferndale Chamber of Commerce,* % Carriage House Antiques, PO Box 1254, Ferndale, California 95536, (707) 786-4086.

The Trinity River Route

*Passing by the Court House the other evening
we heard considerable noise and upon
opening the hall door discovered that Peter
Paulsen's black cow had been shut in.
Supposing that Pete had placed her there as an
additional guard to county treasury, we
quietly closed the door and passed on.*

Trinity Journal, *November 18, 1871*

California Office of Tourism

Having achieved the dubious distinction of being the most populous state in the nation, finding a truly backroad getaway is almost a thing of the past in California. The one major exception is Trinity County, a stunningly scenic region shadowed by the peaks of the Klamath Mountain range. Here, within an area that spans 3,222 square miles, there is a population of only 14,000, providing plenty of elbow room for RVers to explore a vast network of backroads, hike beautiful mountain trails, fish in some of California's finest lakes and streams, explore a rich historical legacy or simply kick back and bask in the fresh mountain air and sunshine. Just one thing, let's keep this to ourselves.

While it is accessible by SR 299 from both the coast and the central valley route of Interstate 5, RVers should be aware that from either direction the drive to Trinity County is often slow, traveling up sometimes steep mountain roads that twist and turn with the contours of the land. Although patience is required for RVers, you'll be happy to know that the route is, for the most part, a well-maintained, two-lane road with an abundance of passing lanes. In the winter months, for obvious reasons, caution is advised during bad weather. During the summer months, keep an eye out for fast-moving logging trucks and deer (both of which often seem to come from nowhere).

Weaverville: Trinity County Seat

Whichever approach you take, I recommend that you start your Trinity visit by taking the time to drive to the county seat of Weaverville. Having had an opportunity to visit Weaverville off and on for the past twenty years, I view the town today with mixed emotions. When I first discovered this little community of 3,000 in 1970, it was a sleepy little mountain town eking out a living from the timber industry and a small tourist trade. If you walked the streets back then, besides loggers and vacationers, you were just as likely to run into the occasional prospector, drifter, and sixties drug-culture dropout.

Today the town, despite being buffeted by a fluctuating timber market, is a thriving community bursting with civic pride. Weaverville bustles with activity aimed at preserving its colorful history and is working hard to prepare for what looks like a bright future as a tourist mecca. Stroll the streets now and you see the smiling faces of retirees who have come here to discover the good life and younger residents who always seem more than willing to answer questions and point visitors in the right direction.

It's gratifying to see some of these changes, but I can't help but be concerned that Weaverville's down-home hospitality might eventually succumb to the commercialism that has gripped some of California's other mountain communities. It would be a shame to see this historically

Tour **2** *60 miles*

WEAVERVILLE • JOSS HOUSE CHINESE TEMPLE • J. J. (JAKE) JACKSON MEMORIAL MUSEUM • TRINITY COUNTY HISTORICAL PARK • TRINITY RIVER • LEWISTON • TRINITY LAKE • LEWISTON LAKE • DOUGLAS CITY • HAYFORK • NATURAL BRIDGE • RUTH LAKE • TRINITY ALPS WILDERNESS

Peaceful Waters.
With 145 miles of unspoiled shoreline, Clair Engle Lake, known to locals as Trinity Lake, is an inviting place to fish, float, or just enjoy the forested panorama.

Two Views of Weaverville.
Unique spiral staircases (*above*), a Weaverville trademark, allowed dual ownership of the commercial structures along Main Street. (*Below*) This colorful and quaint nineteenth-century home does modern-day duty serving Trinity County visitors as the Mustard Seed Café.

significant hamlet join the ranks of trendy tourist traps whose streets are lined with arts and crafts shops, high-priced antique stores, and restaurants that specialize in quiche and crêpes. In a town where you can still get reliable tips on where the big ones are biting, advice on the right fly pattern for casting in the nearby rivers and streams, or a hearty steak dinner with french fries and a slice of homemade apple pie for dessert, one hopes it will stay that way.

Your first stop should be the Trinity County Chamber of Commerce office at 317 Main Street to pick up the latest information on special events. You'll also find a host of pamphlets and mimeographed materials on local attractions and historical sites for Weaverville and the surrounding communities.

It was a gold strike that brought a flood of settlers into the Trinity region in 1848 and laid the foundations for the founding of Weaverville two years later. According to legend, Weaverville began as a tent city established by three miners — James Howe, John Weaver, and Daniel Bennett — who had come to try their luck in the gold fields and decided the area was the ideal place to put down roots. After completing work on a small cabin on July 8, 1850, the three decided it was time to pick a name for their fledgling town. They drew straws, with John Weaver coming up the winner.

Begin your tour of Weaverville by taking a stroll along Main Street where you can admire the well-restored buildings and read the historical markers affixed to some of the storefronts. The spiral staircases that wind from the sidewalk to the second floor on a few of the buildings here will be sure to pique your curiosity. The staircases date back to Weaverville's early days when it was common to have different owners for the first and second floors of a building.

Besides the old storefronts of Main Street, Weaverville's most striking structure is the Joss House Chinese Temple, at the corner of Main and Oregon streets, now maintained as a state historic site. The ornate blue and brown building, decorated in gold leaf, was erected in the 1850s by Chinese immigrants who came to work the Trinity gold fields. At the height of the gold rush here the Joss House served as the religious center for some 2,500 Chinese residents of the area. It is still in use today as a sacred temple, but guided tours are offered by state park rangers.

From the Joss House it's just a few steps east on Main Street to the J. J. (Jake) Jackson Memorial Museum and Trinity County Historical Park. Displays include a variety of artifacts from the early life of Weaverville and the surrounding area; there are Indian relics, old bottles, a restored jail cell, a complete blacksmith shop, numerous photographs of Trinity County life, an 1849 hand-pump fire engine, and a number of exhibits relating the history of the Chinese during the gold rush. Throughout the museum and its grounds there are also a number of examples of old mining equipment. The restored stamp mill, used in the mining process, is in a separate building next to the museum and is operational; demonstrations are held throughout the summer.

If you head back west on Main Street for about two blocks you'll come to the Weaverville Bandstand. Erected in 1902, the bandstand was the culmination of efforts by Weaverville citizens to find a home for their local band, which has performed on this site, the town plaza, since 1877. Today the bandstand is still used for summer concerts and the town's Fourth of July celebration.

"The Weaverville Brass Band is certainly as good as can be found short of the cities. The members of the band take great pride in perfecting themselves, and within the past two months have very much improved their execution, under the direction of their talented leader J. E. Sedlak."
Trinity Journal, *July 5, 1856*

Old-time Bandstand.
Erected near the turn of the century, the Weaverville Bandstand is a source of cultural pride for the citizens of this mountain community.

Lewiston Landmark.
A time-worn little red pioneer school-house is a well-preserved relic of Lewiston's early days.

Rest in Peace.
Many of the farmers, miners, and cattlemen who contributed to the history of Lewiston were laid to rest in the Lewiston Pioneer Cemetery, established in 1850.

From Weaverville you're free to follow your interests to the four corners of the county. I suggest anglers take SR 299 west to the point where it overlooks the Trinity River Gorge. Along this stretch of river you'll find several campgrounds with trails leading down to the river. Trout fishing throughout the summer is usually very good and the steelhead fishing in the fall can be some of the best in the state.

Fishing and Sightseeing in Lewiston

In addition to the stretch of river west of Weaverville, there is also excellent fishing along the Trinity River east of town. One of my favorite spots is the fly-fishing-only stretch in nearby Lewiston, reached by taking SR 3 north from Weaverville to Rush Creek Road (a distance of seventeen miles), or SR 299 east to the Lewiston turnoff, at Browns Mountain Road. In past years I have taken some nice browns and rainbows here and return as often as I can to fish this part of the river that extends from the old Lewiston bridge to the base of Lewiston Dam. Unfortunately, the fishing in recent years has not been as good here because state officials have increased the water flow from the dam to enhance the fall salmon run. While those efforts have paid off, with salmon now swimming all the way up to the dam to spawn, the higher water level has diminished the fly-fishing. Still, for uncrowded fishing, this part of the Trinity is superb.

While you're in Lewiston take some time to explore the side streets and historic sites of this picturesque hamlet, founded by ferryboat operator B.F. Lewis in 1855. Despite early predictions that Lewiston would become an important town in the Klamath Mountain region, the community has never grown much beyond the 588 people who had settled there by 1880.

The sites of interest here are the old Lewiston Hotel located on Deadwood Road, the Lewiston church built in 1895 and still standing at the corner of Church Lane and Goose Ranch Road, the Little Red School-house, built in 1862, on Goose Ranch Road, and the single-lane Lewiston Bridge that spans the Trinity River on Turnpike Road. I recommend taking the short walk from the old schoolhouse to the Lewiston Pioneer Cemetery at the corner of Goose Ranch and Lewiston roads. This cemetery was established in 1850 and many prominent Lewiston settlers have been laid to rest on this small hill that overlooks the river. A historical plaque in the cemetery honors the miners, farmers, and cattlemen who contributed to the early history of the area.

Further Explorations of Trinity

Douglas City

From Lewiston you can continue your quest of Trinity County history by backtracking to SR 299 and turning west to Douglas City. Now little more than a wide spot in the road, Douglas City was the location of one of the richest gold strikes in Trinity County in the 1850s. As a stop on the stagecoach line, it was also near here that the following drama, later reported in the *Trinity Journal*, was played out:

A highwayman rose from behind a large rock by the roadside and drawing a fine-sight on the messenger demanded the Wells Fargo & Co.'s treasure box. The robber having the drop on him, John McNemer, the messenger, very reluctantly passed out the box, and in obedience to orders from the "Knight of the Road," Charlie Williams, the driver drove on. Having got out of sight around a point, the stage stopped and McNemer getting off went back over the point and suddenly came upon the robber who was busily engaged in opening the box with an old pick. It was now McNemer's turn, and raising his shotgun he fired one barrel which, hitting the robber, made him stagger, and to be sure of his game McNemer then fired the other barrel; this also hit the robber and killed him instantly.

Hayfork's Natural Bridge

Douglas City is noteworthy now primarily because it marks the turnoff to SR 3, and the narrow, winding route to the town of Hayfork. First settled in 1851, Hayfork began as Kingsbury, later changed to Hay Town, and finally to Hayfork in recognition of its location on the north fork of the south fork of the Trinity River. Like many of the other towns in the county, Hayfork was a mining town in its early days, but it owes much of its success and staying power as one of the major communities (population 3,000) in Trinity County to its setting in a broad river valley that makes it ideal for ranching and farming.

The trip to Hayfork is worth the twenty miles of slow mountain driving in order to view the nearby Natural Bridge, a limestone arch that crosses a narrow ravine, aptly named Bridge Gulch. The natural limestone arch, which is about 100 feet wide and 50 feet high, with an archway that spans 200 feet, was a popular gathering spot for settlers in Hayfork Valley who often came here for picnics. The names and dates of many of those early pioneers are still legible in a number of carvings in the limestone.

The Natural Bridge was also the site of one of the more violent episodes in Trinity County history. The Bridge Gulch Massacre occurred in the summer of 1852 and was sparked by the killing of a Weaverville citizen, Colonel J.R. Anderson, by a band of Wintu Indians.

While immediate reports of the killing led settlers in the area to believe the murder of Anderson was a cold-blooded act, a later account by Isaac Cox, a Hayfork resident, noted: "Faithful to truth, we must state that rumor charges the Indians with entertaining a well-founded grudge against the Colonel, and that their hostile demeanor originated in this way."

Be that as it may, Cox, reflecting the frontier view of justice, added: "Be this true or not, the rascals had committed a glaring infraction into the peace and security of the county, and to chastise them was proper and laudable. A company was accordingly made up in Weaverville consisting of about forty men, led by Sheriff Dixon. . . ."

Bureau of Reclamation

Gentle River.
Bordered by lush forest lands, the magnificent Trinity River follows a generally gentle course as it flows from the mountains westward to the Pacific Ocean.

Within hours of the killing, Dixon and his men were in hot pursuit of the Indians and quickly caught up with them at their encampment in Bridge Gulch. Waiting until dawn to attack, the party of settlers camped nearby for the night, then surrounded the Indian settlement of about 150 men, women, and children and launched their attack the following morning. Caught by surprise, the Wintus had little chance to defend themselves, and, by the time the smoke cleared, the only survivors were three children. There were no casualties among Sheriff Dixon's party.

A detailed brochure and map that leads you step by step through the Bridge Gulch Massacre Site can be obtained at the Hayfork Ranger Station, just east of town. Walking the now-peaceful site of this black day in the history of the county, you can't help but be overwhelmed by the thoughts of the violence that occurred here.

While such historical vignettes are reason enough for RVers to indulge in some backroad exploration here, it is the scenery and outdoor recreation opportunities that continue to lure visitors back to these mountains long after they have become familiar with Trinity County history.

On to Trinity Lake

For further exploration of the southern reaches of the county, I recommend continuing along SR 3 south out of Hayfork to the junction of SR 36. At that point turn west and follow the road as it winds through the little town of Forest Glen and into the community of Mad River. Just east of town, take CR 501, which cuts southeast and follows the Mad River to the county's second largest body of water, Ruth Lake.

Fed by the waters of the Mad River, Ruth Lake offers thirty miles of forested shoreline and a peaceful setting with five uncrowded camp-

Backcountry Trails.
Windswept valleys and beautiful mountain vistas await those who leave the comfort of their RV behind and take to the backcountry trails.

Water Sports.
Trinity Lake, ringed by forests and a wide choice of campgrounds, offers some of the best water recreation opportunities to be found in all of northern California.

grounds either on the river bank or the lake shore. The locals here told me that the lake offers especially good fishing for rainbow trout, with twenty-inchers quite common. Largemouth bass and catfish are also said to be abundant.

For those in the county's northern regions, I suggest taking SR 3 north from Weaverville, or Trinity Center Road north out of Lewiston, both of which climb into the Trinity Alps region along a route that loops up and around the beautiful Trinity and Lewiston lakes.

Although it has been officially designated Clair Engle Lake in honor of a state political figure, to residents of the county who stubbornly refuse to accept that designation the huge body of water that spreads out from the foothills of the Trinity Alps will always be known as Trinity Lake. This lake, the largest in the county, is 20 miles long, with 145 miles of shoreline and more than twenty campgrounds nestled in the forests along the shore. As you drive the mountain roads around the lake you'll find a number of vantage points that offer excellent overviews of Trinity Lake's deep blue waters, which stretch fingerlike into the recesses and valleys of the Klamath Mountains. Despite the inviting setting, the campgrounds in the spring and fall — the ideal time for fishing these waters — are often nearly deserted. During the summer you're likely to find the campgrounds full on holiday weekends, but the chances are good there will be plenty of sites left at other times.

Formed behind a 538-foot-high earthfill dam, Trinity Lake is kept at a relatively constant level year-round, with a water surface elevation that is about 2,337 feet above sea level. What is especially interesting about this lake is that, in spite of its elevation and cool mountain setting, the surface temperature during the summer months runs as high as 75°, making it an ideal spot for swimming and water skiing.

Bigfoot Country.
Cascading clear mountain streams originate in the high, snow-capped peaks of Bigfoot Country.

Up a Lazy River.
A warm summer day and a lazy river provide an irresistible combination for youngsters.

RV Adventure.
Rugged, dramatic Trinity County is an ideal place to enjoy the vast array of nature's beauty from a home on wheels.

Of course, Trinity Lake's main attraction is its fishing, and it has gained a reputation for producing record bass, as well as excellent fishing for catfish, rainbow and German brown trout, and kokanee salmon. In 1976 a California record nine-pound-one-ounce smallmouth bass was taken here. The proprietor of the bait and tackle store in Weaverville told me that largemouth bass in excess of ten pounds are not uncommon.

If, like me, you're partial to trout fishing, head downstream from Trinity Lake to the waters of Lewiston Lake. This, the third largest lake in the county, spreads out for eight miles from the base of the Trinity Dam to the Lewiston Dam just above the town of Lewiston. The consistently low temperatures of the lake, resulting from deep-water inflow from Trinity Lake, make Lewiston's water unsuitable for swimming and other water sports such as water skiing. However, the lake's cool water, which ranges from 40° to 67° at the surface, provides an ideal habitat for rainbows, browns, and eastern brook trout.

You can have good luck here simply casting into the narrow lake from the shore, or, for even better results, try casting a fly from a drifting boat. Lakeside residents here told me the fly-fishing is best on Lewiston in the spring and fall months. They also told me that rainbow and brown trout over eighteen inches are quite common. A trophy brown weighing more than twenty-five pounds, and just two ounces shy of the state record, was taken from this lake a few years ago.

Stalking Bigfoot

In addition to going after record trout and bass, RVers who come to Trinity County should take the opportunity to try their luck at tracking down the legendary Bigfoot. The best way to do that is to strike out on a day hike or overnight backpacking excursion into the backcountry.

Alpine Lakes.
Pristine alpine lakes abound in the rugged Trinity Alps Wilderness Area where winter lingers late into the summer.

There are any number of excellent day-hike trails located throughout the county and the people at the chamber office in Weaverville can steer you to some of the best with their list of suggested routes. I recommend you try the Swift Creek Trail, reached by taking the Swift Creek Road (check locally for current road conditions) out of the town of Trinity Center. This is a fairly easy hike that takes you back into a primitive area that passes through timber and meadows to the rim of the Swift Creek Gorge. The scenery is spectacular; don't forget your camera.

Fly-Fishers' Heaven.
A special "fly-fishing" section of the Trinity River offers an opportunity to tangle with lunker brown and rainbow trout.

For an easy walk that offers an opportunity to spend a leisurely day in the woods, try the Stoddard/McDonald Lake Trail, located at the extreme north end of Trinity Lake, just off SR 3 near the Coffee Creek Ranger Station. This hike is only about three miles long and winds through thick forest and lush meadows, some of the county's most beautiful backcountry. Pack a picnic lunch and enjoy.

For those in good shape who really want to get away from it all, a backpacking trip into the Trinity Alps Wilderness is an experience that you won't forget. A few years ago my son and I packed into this rugged backcountry in late June over trails that were still snow covered in spots. In the space of two days we climbed steep trails to break out into a narrow valley where we pitched our tent on the shores of an alpine lake, in the shadows of the jagged peaks of the mountains. In the daytime we fished the lakes for pan-sized trout and explored some of the trails that climb the steep mountain slopes and cut back into the thick timber. At night we cooked the trout over an open fire and shared the campsite with curious deer who wandered in at dusk looking for a handout. We never did spot Bigfoot, but we came away with enough memories to last a lifetime.

POINTS OF INTEREST: California Tour 2

The Trinity River Route

[Map of The Trinity River Route showing Clair Engle Lake, Trinity Dam, Lewiston Lake, Lewiston Dam, Lewiston, Weaverville, Trinity River, Douglas City, Hayfork, Mad River, Forest Glen, Ruth Lake, and highways 3, 5, 36, and 299]

0   10MI
0   20KM

ACCESS: SR 299, via US 101 at Arcata or I-5 at Redding.

INFORMATION: *Trinity County Chamber of Commerce,* 317 Main Street, P.O. Box 517, Weaverville, California 96093, (916) 623-6101.

ANNUAL EVENTS:
Hayfork: *Old-fashioned Independence Day,* July; *Trinity County Fair,* August.

Trinity Center: *Fly-in Barbecue and Arts and Crafts Faire,* September.

Weaverville: *Chinese New Year Celebration,* February; *Fourth of July Celebration, Arts and Crafts Faire,* July; *Harvest Moon Festival,* Oct.

MUSEUMS:
Weaverville: *J. J. (Jake) Jackson Memorial Museum,* on Main Street, (916) 623-5211, call for hours; *Joss House State Historic Park,* Oregon and Main Streets, (916) 623-5284. Year-round, tours in summer.

RESTAURANTS:
Hayfork: *Alice's Restaurant,* Highway 3 and Hyampom Road, (916) 628-4212; American.
   Weaverville: *The Brewery,* 401 South Main Street, (916) 623-3000; American. *The Mustard Seed Café,* 252 Main Street, (916) 623-2922; breakfast and lunch. *Trinity Alps Golf & Country Club,* SR 299 to Glenn Road, to Fairway Drive, (916) 623-5411; Continental.

Northern Gold Country

The snow lay deep on the Sierras, and every mountain creek became a river, and every river a lake. Each gorge and gulch was transformed into a tumultuous watercourse that descended the hillsides, tearing down giant trees and scattering its drift and debris along the plain. " . . . Water put the gold in them gulches," said Stumpy.

Bret Harte, *The Luck of Roaring Camp*

F or me, California's northern Gold Country — that stretch from Auburn to Sierraville along historic SR 49 — represents one of the RVer's best backroads opportunities. Although this section of the famed route of the forty-niners boasts some of the state's most magnificent scenery and some of the most well-preserved remnants of the gold rush era, it remains a truly unhurried travel experience. Unfortunately, there are signs that may be changing as more and more residents of the region recognize there's still gold in thar hills in the form of tourist dollars. So if you want to really see this section of forty-niner country in all its unspoiled splendor, I suggest you hurry.

Going for the Gold

What makes this route especially appealing for RVers is the fact that there are few large towns along the route that offer overnight hotel accommodations. However, campgrounds abound, some private, but the vast majority are U.S. Forest Service facilities set in spectacular scenic locales on the banks of the south, middle and north forks of the Yuba River. Thus RVers can linger in the region, leisurely taking in the sites or simply enjoying the backcountry solitude.

Auburn's Unique Story

Like all the towns in the Mother Lode, Auburn, situated where I-80 intersects SR 49, has its own unique story in gold-rush history. Located just twenty miles north of Coloma, the site where James Marshall unearthed the first gold at Sutter's Mill, Auburn began as a mining camp when miners hit pay dirt just four months after that initial gold strike. In fact, Auburn — then known as North Fork Dry Diggings — is said to have been an especially rich source of ore, yielding between $1,000 to $1,500 per day per miner. More than $75 million was taken from the Auburn region between 1848 and 1855.

Unlike other towns in the area, though, Auburn continued to prosper after the gold ran out. In less than a decade after the first digging began, the town's emphasis on gold began to wane, and it gradually emerged as a trading center for the northern mines. By 1865 its importance as a hub of commerce was assured when Auburn became a stop on the Central Pacific Railroad. Before the railroad arrived, Auburn did earn the dubious distinction of launching the fine art of stagecoach robbery. History has it that the first stagecoach holdup occurred here, an enterprise that caught on quickly and became a major growth industry in the years before the turn of the century.

Today many of the reminders of Auburn's gold-rush past are gradually being swallowed by the town's continued growth. For those who want to

Tour **3**
Side trip to Rough and Ready, 5 miles

AUBURN • GRASS VALLEY • NEVADA CITY • ROUGH AND READY • MALAKOFF DIGGINS STATE HISTORICAL PARK • NORTH BLOOMFIELD • NORTH SAN JUAN • CAMPTONVILLE • SHENNANIGAN FLATS CAMPGROUND • DOWNIEVILLE • SIERRA CITY • SIERRA BUTTES • GRAEAGLE • PLUMSA-EUREKA STATE PARK • JOHNSVILLE

Prospecting for Paydirt.
In waters once worked by more primitive means, modern-day prospectors use a gas-powered dredge to work the gravel of the Yuba River.

Empire Mine.
Now a state historic park, the Empire Mine was once the richest producing mine in California. During more than 100 years of operation it yielded nearly 6 million ounces of gold.

trace some of the history here I suggest a stop at the chamber of commerce (1101 High Street), where you can pick up *The Guide to Auburn's Old Town.* That will direct you to the few historical buildings that remain, such as the old post office and the Wells Fargo Office. You'll also be directed to the Placer County Museum, which contains many pieces of old mining equipment and exhibits on early Indian cultures and life in the gold fields.

Grass Valley and Nevada City

From Auburn, SR 49 heads north for about twenty-four miles on a fairly straight, wide road to the twin towns of Grass Valley and Nevada City. Combined, these two historic mining towns now have a population of more than 10,000 and are losing much of their former charm to growth as lumbering centers and an increasing popularity as retirement communities. But both Grass Valley and Nevada City do retain some ties to the past, and it's worth pausing here to explore a few of those remnants.

As it is today, Grass Valley was a bustling community back in the gold-rush days. This was the site of big mining operations by the major companies who built the Empire, North Star, Brunswick and other mines. These ambitious mining operations dug miles of tunnels and shafts beneath both towns and many of these deep mines remained active well into the 1950s.

I found the best way to get a real sense of what these major mining operations were like was to stop off at the Empire Mine (1½ miles east of SR 49 on Empire Street), which has been maintained as a state historic park since its acquisition in 1975. There are more than 700 acres here that include some well-preserved old buildings like the Empire Cottage, the machine shop, and a number of others in varying states of decay. An interesting film relates the mines' histories and illustrates some of the

Street of Memories.
Although now struggling between the forces of the past and the present, Grass Valley, one of the most important towns of the Northern Mines, retains much of its early charm.

Nevada City.
Despite the fact that it is now intersected by a modern freeway, Nevada City manages to retain its links to the past with well-preserved architecture and quaint touches such as old-fashioned buggy rides.

mining processes that yielded 5.8 million ounces of gold during the Empire's 106 years of operation.

While touring the park, the ranger suggested that if I wanted a more detailed glimpse of the region's mining operations and history I should stop at the Pelton Wheel Mining Museum, located a short distance away at the end of South Mill Street. This museum, generally said to be the best in the Mother Lode, houses the massive (largest in the world) Pelton wheel, which was used to power mining equipment, as well as a number of other gold-field artifacts.

Of course, no visit here is complete without driving by the home of Grass Valley's most famous resident, Lola Montez. At the time of my visit the home (on the corner of Mill and Walsh streets) had been restored and designated as a state and national monument, but was not open to the public. Born Eliza Gilbert in Ireland, Lola came to the gold country after becoming a rather notorious figure in Europe. She traveled to the United States with the intention of entertaining in the dance halls and saloons of San Francisco. But the people in that city didn't think much of her talents, particularly her "Spider Dance," which featured rubber spiders shaken out of her dress as she gyrated across the stage.

So Lola took her act on the road and ended up in the gold camps where the less discerning miners gave her an enthusiastic welcome. For a time she settled down in Grass Valley with her pet monkey and grizzly bear and became the talk of the town. History has it that she led a fast life here, giving lavish parties and generally scandalizing the local, more sedate, God-fearing citizens. Finally, things became too tame for Lola and she moved on to entertain in Australia and New York (where she died at the young age of forty-three).

Firehouse No. 2.
With fire being an ever-present threat to early gold-rush communities, Nevada City's old Firehouse No. 2 was one of the town's most important structures.

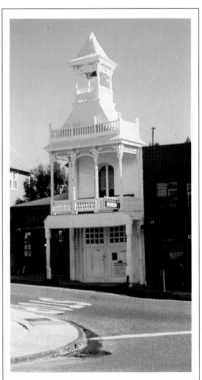

Assay Office.
Historic Ott's Assay Office houses the Nevada City Mint and is next door to the chamber of commerce office where visitors can get detailed information on walking tours of the town.

Nevada City Chamber of Commerce

Regal Victorian.
Walk or drive Nevada City's side streets and find some of the best-restored examples of Victorian architecture in the northern Mother Lode.

Nevada City Chamber of Commerce

Just a couple of miles over the hill from Grass Valley you'll enter Nevada City, a town with a distinctly different character than its neighbor and one that has been likened to an "old aristocratic, once-wealthy lady now living in reduced circumstances." It's an apt description for this hilly, quaint Victorian community. Many picturesque old homes are scattered throughout the town. Viewing them is not easy for motorhome drivers, however, since the steep hills and narrow streets make maneuvering difficult, but an interesting walking tour is offered.

I suggest you park your rig and pick up a walking tour map at the Nevada City Chamber of Commerce (132 Main Street). From the chamber office you can take in Ott's Assay Office right next door, then continue on to the old hotels and red brick firehouse on Broad Street. In the old Chinese section on Commercial Street a few well-preserved period buildings remain. A stop at the American Victorian Museum on Spring Street not only provides an opportunity to view art and artifacts of the gold-rush era, but also gives you an opportunity to have lunch since this unique museum also houses a restaurant.

Rough and Ready

Before returning to SR 49, the folks at the chamber of commerce office urged me to take the time to drive the five miles out to Rough and Ready, a hamlet located just west of Grass Valley on SR 20. Although the town is considerably diminished from the 2,000 souls who occupied it during its heyday in the 1850s, I was glad I made the trip, if only to hear about the town's colorful past.

Liquid Refreshment.
Travelers along scenic SR 49 will find plenty of places where they can pause to enjoy the view, some of which even offer a drink from a cool mountain spring.

The band of Mexican War veterans who settled here in 1848 paid tribute to their commanding officer, General Zachary Taylor, by naming the town in honor of his nickname, "Old Rough and Ready." Living up to its image as a community of stalwart, independent men and women, just two years later the town officially seceded from the United States in protest over a federal miner's tax. A few months later, when the citizens decided they wanted to have a post office in town, the government told them one could not be built since they were no longer part of the United States. Satisfied that they had made their point, they rejoined the Union on July 4, 1840.

On the Trail of the Forty-Niners

Back on the main highway, just north of Nevada City the route of the forty-niners makes a sharp left at the junction of SR 49 and SR 20. From this point on, the road really takes on a backroad appearance as it heads deeper into the Tahoe National Forest and winds toward the south fork of the Yuba River. About seven miles from the turn you'll want to gear down for a sharp descent toward the river. I found it was also necessary to take it slow along this stretch because it's a popular gathering spot for weekenders from Sacramento who come here to swim in the Yuba's clear blue waters and sunbathe on the rocks along the shore.

North San Juan

After rolling slowly across the river's narrow bridge, I accelerated sharply for the long climb out of the river canyon up to an open area that widens out into private ranch lands. From here the road winds along toward the village of North San Juan. About a mile before the town you'll come to the road that heads east to Malakoff Diggins State Historic Park and the little restored town of North Bloomfield. This is an especially interesting stop because it allows a closeup look at a major hydraulic mining operation that ravaged the countryside here and changed the landscape forever. And North Bloomfield, with several historic structures, is worth a closer look. Just outside of town there is a thirty-unit campground.

Introduced to the gold fields in 1853 by Nevada City miner E. E. Matteson, hydraulic mining utilized tremendous jets of water forced through enormous steel nozzles to wash the earth into a system of flumes and ditches. As the water flowed through these often elaborate systems of channels, the heavier gold would fall to the bottom of the flume while the lighter soil would be carried off, usually to be deposited in the river channel. This was an extremely effective method of working large areas of land in a short amount of time. Its efficiency as a gold producer, however, is debatable. One thing is certain: Hydraulic mining, very popular in the northern mines, was enormously destructive. The reminders of its destructive force can be found here in the form of large piles of rock left deposited near the banks of nearly every waterway.

That destruction is also recorded in the history of North San Juan, which was devastated one year by a spring flood, the direct result of hydraulic mining operations that altered the river channel and sent the Yuba flowing through the heart of the town. Although North San Juan was rebuilt after the flood, today very little remains here except for a few old homes, some ancient buildings in varying states of disrepair, a gas station, and a general store. What is most interesting is the old cemetery that sits atop a hill at the south edge of town. I suggest you take the time to park along the side road near the cemetery and walk up the asphalt service road and through the gates. Here you'll find a number of headstones dating back to the gold-rush days. Among the modest headstones, chipped and worn smooth by time, there are some fairly grand-looking monuments, now also considerably weathered, attesting to the wealth and stature of some of North San Juan's early residents.

Just north of town, SR 49 descends gradually toward the middle fork of the Yuba. After you cross the river, there is a sharp turn to the right on a narrow little access road that leads down to a covered bridge and into a

Boot Hill.
Inscriptions on the weathered tombstones in the Mother Lode cemeteries tell the tale of hardship and violence that faced those who came here to seek their fortune.

Yuba River.
Enclosed by steep, forested canyons, the cascading North Fork of the Yuba River is popular with both anglers and prospectors.

Forest Service campground. An interesting story centers on the bridge, which was washed out during a spring flood in the late 1800s. When the residents of the area retrieved the bridge downstream and put it back in place, they found it did not fit exactly as it had before. It was only after they had finished restoring the bridge that they discovered it had been switched end for end.

Camptonville

Leaving the middle fork of the Yuba, the ascent is gradual as the road winds up through a series of curves and then straightens out to run along a plateau that offers excellent views across the heavily forested valley far below. A few miles up the road you'll see a sign noting the turnoff for Camptonville, another old mining town in which some of the buildings have been restored. A number of residents remain, although Camptonville is only a shadow of its glory days when 1,500 residents dwelt among its hills and along its side streets. There is an amusing monument at the west end of town erected in memory of William "Bull" Meek, a stagecoach driver and Wells Fargo agent who was responsible for getting supplies to the mining camps in the gold country. While that job was important, legend has it that Bull earned the undying respect and gratitude of the miners because it was his stage that regularly brought supplies to the bordello in nearby Downieville.

Shennanigan Flats

From Camptonville on, SR 49 becomes exceptionally scenic as the highway goes deeper into heavy forest and then begins a very sharp drop to the breathtaking beauty of the canyon that holds the north fork of the Yuba. As you cross the river here, keep an eye out for a left turn at the north end of the bridge. This turn takes you onto a narrow one-lane dirt road that hugs the cliff above the river. If you follow the road for about two miles, it leads back into a campground that has been given the whimsical name of Shennanigan Flats. It's a very small facility that sits partially atop a plateau about thirty feet above the river, and it's a tight squeeze for large motorhomes and trailers. During the height of the summer season I wouldn't recommend driving back to the campground because chances are it will be full and maneuvering to turn around is difficult.

I was lucky enough to find a spot for the night (no hookups). I had just enough time to get settled and still have enough daylight to cast a fly in the Yuba. Walking about 300 yards downstream I came to a couple of large, azure-green pools formed by the backwash of water rushing over huge boulders rising out of the middle of the river. Looking downstream I could see a few big trout holding close to the banks and with just two casts I hooked a nice twelve-inch rainbow. It tasted pretty good that night cooked over the coals in my campsite fire pit.

Talking to others in the campground that evening I learned that my luck was nothing out of the ordinary. In fact, I was told, the fishing all along the Yuba's north fork is excellent. I learned also that this section of the river is very popular with prospectors, whose luck seems almost as good as the anglers. I was told of people who found nuggets by simply panning the gravel on the river bank, and even bigger nuggets being brought up by the prospectors who worked the river bottom with gas-operated dredges.

Another thing I learned is that, unlike a fisherman, you don't ask a

Sierra Buttes.
One of the highest points in this region, the rugged Sierra Buttes, snowcapped year-round, are a majestic landmark for travelers north of Sierra City.

Looking for Color.
In the cold, clear waters of the upper reaches of the Yuba River's north fork, an RVing prospector uses a sluice to work the river bed for gold.

prospector if he is having any luck. I put that question to a couple of grizzled-looking veterans who were shoveling gravel into a sluice not too far from the campground. They fixed me with an icy stare and mumbled, "We're doin' all right."

Later I related this story to a fellow camper who had some prospecting equipment at his campsite, and he laughed, telling me: "Prospectors don't like to talk about how much gold they're takin' out, 'cause they're not exactly eager to pay taxes on their earnings. A lot of 'em think someone might turn them into the IRS." I thought back to those rugged folks in Rough and Ready who seceded from the Union over the miner's tax, and decided times hadn't changed all that much.

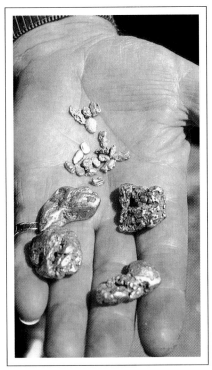

Placer Gold.
Shaped by rushing water and tumbling rocks, glistening nuggets of placer gold are some of the more impressive samples taken from the rivers and streams of the Northern Mine country.

Downieville

I had a chance to learn even more about the modern prospector's character the next day when I rolled into Downieville, some fifteen miles north of the turnoff to Shennanigan Flats. Incidentally, along this stretch of highway before reaching the city limits of Downieville, you'll pass several Forest Service campgrounds, a couple located on the banks of the Yuba, and one set up on a hill overlooking the highway and the river. The view makes a stop at one of these campgrounds very inviting as this stretch of the Yuba is breathtaking. All along this section of the Yuba the water cascades over huge rocks, forming pools that range from deep blue to turquoise as it rushes in an awesome torrent parallel to the highway.

I arrived in Downieville in time to do some shopping at a flea market set up in the heart of town. Here about a half-dozen peddlers, most of them full-time prospectors, offered vials of souvenir gold dust, small nuggets, and an array of gold jewelry made from shiny placer nuggets. One bearded, weathered-looking individual dressed in faded, blue bib overalls had a glass display case that, besides holding some attractive pieces of jewelry, contained a number of nuggets of very impressive size. I asked if he could hold a few of these in his hand so I could get a photo. He was more than happy to oblige, dropping several sizable chunks into his palm. I took a few frames then stepped back to get a picture of him with the nuggets. At that, he put his hand over his face and said, "No, no you can't take my picture. If my ex-wife saw that she'd know where to find me." I agreed to let him keep his secret.

If Downieville has a few such characters among its present population of just under 400, it no doubt had even more when it was a booming mining town just after gold was discovered here in 1849. That first strike

News of the North.
The *Mountain Messenger*, Downieville's historic newspaper, still brings the news of the Mother Lode to the residents and visitors on a weekly basis.

Gold Panning.
Gold panning is something that can be enjoyed by prospectors of all ages, with each having an equal chance to strike it rich.

occurred at the site where the Yuba and Downie rivers meet in the middle of town. By June, 1850, Downieville's population had swelled to 5,000 as miners poured in to work the rich deposits along both rivers. Stories of just how rich the claims were are legion. It is said that one sixty-square-foot claim yielded $12,000 in just eleven days, and one site, "Tin Cup Diggings," was so rich that the miners were able to fill a tin cup with gold dust every day. None of those compare, though, to the incredible luck of one miner who unearthed a nugget that weighed just over twenty-five pounds!

Of all the stories about Downieville, however, the one that will linger after all the tales of riches are forgotten is that of Juanita, the dance hall girl who stabbed a miner to death during a saloon argument. Juanita claimed it was self-defense and there was, in fact, some evidence to indicate she was telling the truth. Nevertheless, the miners quickly convened a court, tried Juanita for murder, found her guilty and, just two hours after the stabbing, hanged her from the bridge that carries SR 49 over the Yuba. Thus, Downieville went down in history as the first town in California ever to hang a woman.

Several years later, Downieville became a bit more civilized and went to the trouble of building an honest-to-goodness gallows to hang James O'Neal, a murderer who was convicted in more conventional court proceedings. That gallows still stands, very well preserved in a shaded corner on the north side of the river, right next to the county courthouse — and, incidentally, within easy view of the prisoners in the county jail. It's a sobering site and one I'm sure that has caused more than one prisoner to reflect on the error of his ways.

Besides the old gallows, several other historic structures remain in Downieville. The old Craycroft Building, a two-story brick building with huge iron doors, stands in the heart of town, now housing a grocery store. The United Methodist Church, built in 1856, is located across the river from the Craycroft Building and is still in excellent condition. Another old building of uncertain origin is located just off SR 49, on the south side of the river, and houses a well-equipped museum whose main attraction is a miniature operating model of a gold stamp mill. Within the museum there is also a potpourri of mining artifacts and historic relics donated by long-time residents.

Sierra City

Driving north out of Downieville, SR 49 takes a sharp turn to the left and falls in alongside the Yuba as it makes a very twisting, but gradual, climb to the next stop on the route, Sierra City. If you watch carefully along this stretch you'll probably spot a number of dredging operations in the river. You'll also see the turnoff for another Forest Service campground that is nestled next to the river.

After a drive of about fifteen miles (a slow drive due to the narrow, winding road) the route slips out from under its tree-shaded canopy and emerges into Sierra City. Like its neighbor just to the south, gold was first discovered here in 1850 and was soon the site of the highly productive Sierra Buttes Mine, which produced some $17 million in gold from a network of tunnels that ran from the edge of the town all the way down to the river. Looking to the north there is a fantastic view of the Sierra Buttes that gave the mine its name. For most of the year these jagged peaks hold snow in their deep crevasses. By fall and all the way through late spring, the buttes are covered with snow and present a magnificent sight when the late afternoon sun slides down their slopes. For the early residents of the little valley below, these peaks represented a very real threat. On more than one occasion — the worst being in 1852 — avalanches rumbled down these mountains and wiped out the homes and buildings below.

We're Still Here.
The Mother Lode area is punctuated with a variety of interesting weathered buildings that reflect the hardy spirit of past and present residents.

Another, and perhaps even more spectacular, view of the Sierra Buttes is offered by a drive up SR 89, which cuts sharply north about eight miles above Sierra City. Before leaving the town, however, you might want to browse through some of the craft shops and art galleries operated by local artisans. For those who might want to stay over, there is a private campground just off the main highway in the heart of town, or the Forest Service has an excellent facility at the east edge of town.

Almost immediately after I turned off SR 49 onto SR 89 and began climbing a steep grade up the mountainside, the Sierra Buttes were once again visible in front of the motorhome, framed against a clear blue sky and appearing so close that I felt I could almost reach out and touch them. Then the road swung away from the buttes as it leveled out and to a more northerly direction toward the town of Graeagle.

Toward Graeagle and Beyond

As I rolled along past thick stands of aspen, I spotted two beautiful alpine lakes — Goose and Gold lakes — shimmering in the mountain sun. Although small clearings at the edge of each lake allow space to park a

Sierra Sunset.
Painted on the canvas of blue skies, the sun sets in brilliant pastel hues over Goose Lake.

High Country.
When winter leaves in late June or early July, the nearby high country of the Sierras beckons RVers.

small RV (up to 30 feet), my motorhome was much too large to maneuver among the trees. I had to be content to stop only briefly to admire the scenery and to talk to a forest ranger who happened to be parked in a nearby turnout. He told me the lakes are not too popular with campers in the summer months because they tend to breed a voracious mosquito population. In the late fall, however, he said the mosquitoes die out and the fishing becomes absolutely superb. For those who have small inflatable boats this would be a perfect stop. Bear in mind, though, that the elevation here is about 7,000 feet and the nights can be nippy.

After saying goodbye to the ranger, I continued on up SR 89 to Graeagle, a tiny resort (there's a fine golf course at the south end of town) and retirement community situated on the banks of the middle fork of the Feather River. For those who come this far the main attraction is the Plumas-Eureka State Park, which contains Johnsville, a partially restored mining town that was originally built in 1870. Also housed in the park (open year-round) are an extensive collection of mining equipment and a museum that contains pictorial exhibits on mining activities. A state-operated campground is within the boundaries of the park.

From Graeagle I backtracked to SR 49 and drove over the Yuba Pass summit (6,701 feet) to Sierraville and the last stretches of 49 because I was curious to see the end of the famous route of the forty-niners.

From Yuba Pass I wound east through the timber of the Tahoe National Forest, alongside the trickling stream that becomes the mighty Yuba's north fork, and dropped down the mountainside into a broad valley where cattle grazed peacefully in lush green fields. Looking down on this pastoral scene I couldn't help thinking about the settlers who came across this valley by wagon and horseback more than a century ago and rode into history as California's forty-niners.

POINTS OF INTEREST: California Tour 3

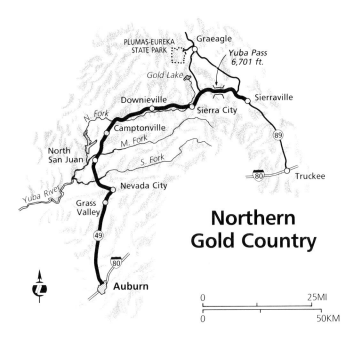

Northern
Gold Country

ACCESS: I-80 to Auburn, north on SR 49.

INFORMATION: *Auburn Area Chamber of Commerce,* 512 Auburn Ravine Road, Auburn, California 95603, (916) 885-5616; *Nevada County Chamber of Commerce,* 248 Mill Street, Grass Valley 95945, (916) 273-4667; *Nevada City Chamber of Commerce,* 132 Main Street, Nevada City, California 95959; (916) 265-2692; *Sierra County Chamber of Commerce,* P.O. Box 36, Downieville, California 95936, (916) 289-3261.

ANNUAL EVENTS:
Auburn: *Homes Tour and Arts Festival,* May; *Auburn District Fair,* June; *Placer County Fair,* July.

Grass Valley: *Bluegrass Festival,* June; *County Fair,* August; *Cornish Christmas Celebration,* December.

Nevada City: *Antique Fair,* May; *Lola Montez Extravaganza,* June; *Butterfly Concert,* August; *Trade Fair,* October; *Artists Christmas Fair,* December.

MUSEUMS:
Auburn: *Placer Gold Country County Museum,* 1273 High Street, (916) 885-9570. Tuesday-Sunday, year-round except major holidays.

Downieville: *Sierra Museum,* on Main Street, (916) 289-3261. Call for hours.

Grass Valley: *Pelton Wheel Mining Museum,* Allison Ranch Road at south end of Mill Street, open daily, (916) 273-4255. May-October. *Lola Montez Home,* on the corner of Mill and Walsh Streets. Daily, year-round, except major holidays.

Nevada City: *American Victorian Museum,* 325 Spring Street, (916) 265-5804. Daily, year-round. *Firehouse Museum,* 214 Main Street, (916) 265-5468. Daily, year-round, except major holidays.

Sierra City: *Kentucky Mine Museum,* via SR 49 one mile northeast of town to Sierra County Historical Park, (916) 862-1310. Wednesday-Sunday, Memorial Day-September; Saturday and Sunday in October.

SPECIAL ATTRACTIONS:
Grass Valley: *Empire Mine State Historic Park,* one mile east of SR 49 at 10791 East Empire Street (916) 273-8522. Daily, year-round; call for hours.

Nevada City: *Malakoff Diggins State Historic Park,* 27 miles northeast off SR 49 on Tyler Foote Road, (916) 265-2740. Daily in summer; Saturday and Sunday only rest of year.

RESTAURANTS:
Auburn: *Butterworth's,* 1522 Lincoln Way, (916) 885-0249; American regional cuisine.

Grass Valley: *Sutter's Mill Restaurant,* 2½ miles south on SR 49 at 13480 SR 49, (916) 273-0388; steak, seafood, prime rib.

Nevada City: *Peter Selaya's California Restaurant,* 320 Broad Street, (916) 265-5697; California cuisine featuring fresh, local foods.

Sierra City: *Herrington's Sierra Pines,* on SR 49, (916) 862-1151; American.

OLD WORLD CHARM
The Wine Country

*Good wine is a good familiar creature
if it be well used.*

William Shakespeare, *Othello, Act II*

Joseph Woods

W ith wineries now dotting the landscape from San Diego to Eureka and the Santa Barbara coast to the western slopes of the Sierra Nevada mountains, it could be said that all of California is now wine country. For dedicated oenophiles, however, California wine country is synonymous with one distinct region — the Napa Valley.

Wine-ing through Napa Valley

Just forty-five miles east of San Francisco on I-80, and less than twenty miles north via SR 37 and SR 128, the Napa Valley boasts nearly 150 wineries in a twenty-five-mile stretch of SR 29 that runs from the community of Napa, northward through Yountville, Oakville, and St. Helena to Calistoga. It isn't sheer numbers alone, though, that have earned Napa Valley the reputation as the state's premier wine-producing region. History, an ideal climate, and a reputation for consistently producing world-class wines have put this bucolic valley on the map.

Like much of California, the Napa Valley awakened during the gold rush when miners poured in, first to work the ridges and streams, and then to seek winter refuge in the valley's mild climate. Although the miners chose not to stay, the favorable setting quickly drew permanent residents — including European immigrants who brought the first grape vines — settling down here to work the rich volcanic soil. The rest, as they say, is history.

The problem is, the history is disputed. According to some, it was Charles Krug, a German fleeing political persecution in his native land, who deserves the credit for founding the valley's wine industry, with the establishment of the first commercial winery in 1861. However, most residents will tell you that it was George Yount (for whom Yountville is named) who set things in motion when he planted the first grapevines here about ten years before Krug's arrival.

Regardless of the Napa Valley's exact history, what is undisputable is that its reputation as a hospitable wine-producing region quickly spread, attracting a steady succession of new vintners. While the valley's growth was understandably slowed by the onset of Prohibition, a number of wineries survived those years by producing sacramental wines and vintages allegedly destined for medicinal purposes. With the end of Prohibition in 1933, the Beringer, Beaulieu, and Mondavi vineyards took the lead in reviving the valley's dormant wine industry. In the 1950s Charles Krug took the innovative step of introducing public tasting. By the 1960s the valley was experiencing a full-blown wine boom as traditional vintners were joined by oil barons and young professionals — engineers, doctors, lawyers — who came here seeking a mid-life career change. In the 1970s Napa Valley wines achieved world-class status when several vari-

Tour **4** *36 miles*

NAPA • ST. HELENA HIGHWAY • SILVERADO TRAIL • OAKVILLE • OAKVILLE GROCERY • ROBERT MONDAVI WINERY • ST. HELENA • FREEMARK ABBEY WINERY • BERINGER RHINE HOUSE • GREYSTONE CELLARS • BALE GRIST MILL STATE HISTORIC PARK • BOTHE NAPA VALLEY STATE PARK • CALISTOGA • SHARPSTEEN MUSEUM

Taste of the Grape.
Nourished by an ideal climate and perfect soil conditions, the vineyards of the Napa Valley yield some of the finest wine grapes in the world.

Joseph Woods

Napa Vineyards.
Enclosed by the Mayacamas and the Howell Mountain ranges, the vineyards here are broken by picturesque wineries and small villages that give the Napa Valley a European identity.

eties won international competitions. Today the remarkable growth continues and, with wineries dotting the landscape throughout this small, verdant valley, the region reigns as the undisputed wine capital of California — if not the country.

Napa Nipping

Referring to the town of Napa, one of the miners who wintered here in 1849 noted, "There isn't any such place. The name got there, but somehow the town hasn't." Well, Napa is very much a reality now, but it serves as a poor introduction to the valley's riches. By and large it is a nondescript community that reigns as the county seat, while having little to do with the wine country just north of the town limits.

A few things, however, do recommend Napa for the RVer. First, especially for traveling families, there is a seemingly endless selection of fast-food chains and other affordable restaurants whose less exotic fare appeals to youngsters. Second, the town has one of the few campgrounds in the area, located at the local fairgrounds. (**Note:** The campground includes full hookups and rates are very reasonable, but sites may not be available during fair events. Call ahead.) Finally, Napa is also a good spot to pick up maps of the valley, as well as up-to-date information on winery tours and the many fine restaurants you'll encounter along the way. An essential is the *Wine Spectator,* a guide (about $3) that lists all the wineries, hours open to the public, and telephone numbers so you can call ahead for information on tours.

Although SR 29 is the primary route north through the valley, there is another north-south route called the Silverado Trail. This narrower road hugs the slopes of the east side of the valley, passing some of the lesser-known wineries as it roams north to link up with SR 29 just above Calistoga. Despite the fact that this route provides a much less crowded and scenic view of the valley, I would recommend beginning your tour on the main highway, taking the occasional opportunity to cross back to the Silverado Trail via one of the many east-west routes along the way.

The Great Wine Way

Driving north on SR 29 — also known as St. Helena Highway (or sometimes whimsically referred to as the Great Wine Way) — the valley quickly widens into open fields and gently rolling hills that are covered by neatly ordered rows of vines. In full leaf under the summer sun the vines are emerald green, in spring, a budding pale green, in autumn, a riot of color, and in winter, barren, gnarled limbs. Obviously, if you're looking for scenic beauty, winters here should be avoided. In autumn, besides the bright colors, the harvest lends an additional air of excitement. I find spring, when the valley and leaves on the vines are awakening, the ideal time for a visit. Predictably, the summer months are when the wineries and restaurants are most crowded, making tours difficult at times. However, the summer season is also the time when valley activities peak.

While the vineyards appear almost immediately after leaving Napa, one can't really count oneself in the valley's wine country until reaching the town of Yountville. Passing a few wineries, I decided to drive on to Yountville, where I paused at the city-park picnic stop long enough to consult the myriad brochures and guide maps obtained at the Napa Chamber of Commerce. Trying to follow the unwritten rule of visiting no more than three wineries in one day, I ran through the dizzying selection in the guide, narrowing down the choices to about a dozen, and then deciding I would hit the road and wing it. Before heading back out, however, I took a few minutes to walk across to the old cemetery and visit George Yount's grave. Again consulting the background material, I ran across the interesting entry that Yount settled here after earning an 11,000-acre land grant for roofing General Vallejo's home in nearby Petaluma. That's a story that should serve as an inspiration to contractors everywhere.

Since a lot of first-time visitors are likely to share my difficulty in deciding exactly which wineries to select as tour possibilities, perhaps a few words about tours in general are appropriate. First, let it be known

Joseph Woods

Ready for Harvest.
Basking in the valley sun, Napa grapes are so rich that one vine can produce as much as one-third of a case of wine.

that I am about as far as you can get from being a wine connoisseur. My knowledge of wine is limited to an occasional glass when dining out. I would venture to say there are a lot of RVers like me who still have a deep appreciation for, and fascination with, the art of wine making.

As for the tours themselves, my experience here left me with the impression that the larger wineries probably offer the neophyte the best and most informative tours. I found that those establishments tended to be well organized and more tolerant of the questions posed by those who are less knowledgeable about the wine-making process. Beyond that, most all of the organized tours (there are some private tours available by reservation only) follow the same agenda of providing a history of the winery itself, showing the various steps to wine making and aging, and then providing an opportunity to sample the winery's products. During the latter, you will, of course, be given an opportunity to purchase a bottle of your favorite grape. However, there is no pressure to buy and the guides will send you on your way with a smile, no doubt hoping you'll have a change of heart and eventually purchase a bottle or two at one of the local retail outlets.

So Much Wine, So Little Time

Having said all that by way of introduction to the tour process, I will now admit that the choice for my first tour, the Robert Mondavi Winery just north of Oakville, was based solely on the fact that the facility offers summertime jazz concerts in conjunction with its tours. While the superb sets by the New Orleans Preservation Hall Jazz Band confirmed the wisdom of my choice, I have to admit that the tour also impressed me as an excellent introduction to wine-country touring.

Built in 1966, the Mondavi Winery, like many of the structures in the valley, looks much older than its years. Its mission-style architecture duplicates the historic structures in California's famous Franciscan mission chain. There is even a churchlike tower that rises above the white stucco building, separating the two main wings of the winery. Interior decor echoes the attempt to capture the valley's Spanish era, and there are a number of magnificent early-California pieces furnishing the tasting and sales room.

For me the highlight of the Mondavi tour, besides the jazz concert on the plush green lawn, was the demonstration of the innovative, experimental equipment designed by the Mondavis and their staff. For example, several motorized horizontal tanks have been installed overhead in the fermenting cellars, designed to rotate continuously. Originally the aim was to keep red wines mixing throughout the fermentation process for maximum color extraction. As it turned out, our guide explained, the tanks didn't accomplish that task. Through further experimentation, however, alternative uses were found for the rotating tanks. Ask the guide to fill you in on the intricacies of these machines.

After the tour, a stop at the tasting room will give you an opportunity to sample the Mondavi vintage-dated Chardonnay and the excellent

Wine and Culture.
The white-walled Robert Mondavi Winery produces both legendary vintages and summer concerts featuring giants of the jazz world.

Joseph Woods

Sauvignon Blanc. The winery is especially proud of its Opus One red table wine, the product of a joint venture with the famous Chateau Mouton-Rothschild winery of Bordeaux, France. I found the Pinot Noir pleasing to my untrained palate, and settled on a bottle for my wine cellar — my rig's cupboard.

From the Mondavi Winery my next stop was St. Helena. Called the unofficial capital of the Napa Valley wine country, because of the dense cluster of some forty wineries surrounding the town, this small community of just over 5,000 offers a surprising number of excellent restaurants (more on that later) as well as a good selection of art galleries, craft, and antique shops. For a change of pace from the winery tours, I recommend a stop at the Hurd Beeswax Candle Factory, located in the Freemark Abbey winery complex about three miles north of town. The candle factory produces an astounding variety of handcrafted candles, most of which are on display in the showroom sales office.

Before heading out of town, however, I strongly urge a stop at the Beringer Vineyards Rhine House, located at the northern outskirts of St. Helena. Again, I have to be honest and say that my decision to stop here was governed less by an appreciation of the Beringer's renown for producing an excellent Cabernet Sauvignon and a rare Cabernet Port, and more by the stunning Old World architecture of the winery's main structure, the Rhine House. Built in 1883 by Frederick Beringer as a replica of his European home, this magnificent home is now the centerpiece of the Beringer tour that begins at the front door and ends in a tasting room magnificently decorated in period style.

In between I encountered one of the wine country's most fascinating curiosities, Beringer's original aging cellars, which consist of 1,000 feet

Napa Chamber of Commerce

Valley Landmark.
Beringer Winery's Rhine House is famed for its wines as well as the elegance of its architecture.

of tunnels dug by Chinese labor in 1876. If you look closely you'll be able to see some of the pick marks still visible in the walls, although in recent years much of the evidence of hand labor has been covered by resurfacing and other recent work that has been done to reinforce the tunnels.

I should also point out to fans of the popular *Falcon Crest* television series that if the Rhine House looks familiar it's not your imagination. However, this is not the house used in the series. The actual location for the television show can be found at the nearby Spring Mountain Vineyards, located a short drive up Spring Mountain Road. The striking resemblance between the two houses is no accident, but rather the result of the desire of this winery's founder, Tiburcio Parrott, to outdo the Beringers with a bigger and better replica of their residence. Because of the winery's newfound stardom, tours here are often crowded and reservations are advised. Some RVs are not allowed at Beringer's, so be sure to call ahead. Also be aware that while the winery tour is free, if you want to tour the Falcon Crest grounds you will be asked to ante up $4 per person.

I elected to pass on the Spring Mountain tour and, instead, drove a few more miles north on SR 29 to the awesome Greystone Cellars operated by the famed Christian Brothers. This imposing structure, which may have made Parrott green with envy, was built in 1889 by mining tycoon William Bourn, spurred by the desire to own the largest stone winery in the world. While Bourn realized his dream for a time, it was hard to find anyone who shared his vision. As a result the huge structure changed hands many times and remained empty for years until the Christian Brothers took it over in 1950.

Tours at this facility start just inside the massive oak doors at the front of the building. Besides getting a chance to glimpse row upon row of

Greystone Cellars.
Imposing Greystone Cellars offers a winery tour featuring a unique corkscrew collection. Now owned by the famed Christian Brothers, it was built in 1889 by mining tycoon William Bourn.

huge oak vats in the dim light of the aging room, a special treat is the unique collection of hundreds of corkscrews assembled by Brother Timothy, one of the first administrators of the winery. The atmosphere of the tasting room, with its stone walls and deeply burnished bar, is special. As you will discover, the Christian Brothers turn out an imposing list of wines, most all of which are available to sample.

Historic Bale Grist Mill

From the Greystone Cellars it's only a few miles north on SR 29 to Bale Grist Mill State Historic Park, one of the valley's few attractions that pre-dates the wine industry. A beautifully preserved structure, the mill was built in 1846 by Dr. Edward Bale to grind wheat harvested from Napa Valley farms. Tours here are largely self-guided, although a ranger is on duty to answer questions. Inside the granary house you'll find two floors of restored mill equipment and displays that demonstrate the business of milling wheat into flour. Outside, a thirty-six-foot waterwheel towers over visitors on the north side of the granary. I recommend the mill as an interesting stop; however, RVers should be aware that parking is limited and they might have to find a spot away from the mill site and walk.

One possibility is located just up the road at Bothe Napa Valley State Park, a scenic, tree-shaded hideaway that features forty campsites accommodating rigs up to thirty-one feet in length. While this park is an extremely desirable spot for RVers to put down some temporary roots, its location right in the heart of the wine country makes it difficult to find a vacancy. In fact when I arrived shortly after noon, mid-week in July, all sites were already booked. The ranger at the gate was kind enough to allow me a quick tour of the facilities, which only heightened my disappointment at not being able to stay.

Aged Oak.
Old oak casks are one of the many methods of aging the wines of the Napa Valley.

Robert E. Howells

Down by the Old Mill Stream.
The historic Bale Grist Mill State Park dates back to the early days of the Napa Valley when it was known more for its wheat fields than its vineyards.

The Past Preserved.
Calistoga's Sharpsteen Museum and Sam Brannan Cottage depart from the region's emphasis on wine to preserve its Old West heritage.

Calistoga: Hot Springs and Mud Baths

After a brief stop at the park I decided to forego further winery tours and drive to the small town of Calistoga at the far end of the valley. Founded in 1860 by flamboyant San Francisco newspaper magnate Sam Brannan, Calistoga's big draw is its natural hot springs and therapeutic mud baths that had drawn visitors to the area long before Brannan arrived on the scene. It was Brannan, though, who saw the riches to be realized from building a spa and vacation retreat to lure wealthy San Franciscans. Legend has it that Brannan bragged he was going to build a retreat that rivaled the famous mineral baths of Saratoga, New York. One night, a tipsy Brannan rose to toast his new spa, which was to be named the Saratoga of California. Instead he raised his glass and announced, "Here's to the Calistoga of Sarafonia." The name stuck.

Those who want to learn about Brannan and the early history of the area should visit the Sam Brannan Cottage and Sharpsteen Museum on Washington Street just off Calistoga's main drag, Lincoln Avenue. The museum, founded by Ben Sharpsteen, a former producer for Disney Studios, houses some Donald Duck and Mickey Mouse displays but is mostly given over to collections that recall the early history of Calistoga and the immediate area. The focal point is a large diorama that stretches the length of one wall and depicts in great detail the heyday of the town. There are also a number of Old West exhibits, including a full-size stagecoach.

Of special interest is the display devoted to Robert Louis Stevenson, who honeymooned on nearby Mount St. Helena in 1880. Later, Stevenson's book, *Silverado Squatters,* was drawn from his impressions of the

Joseph Woods

Mount St. Helena.
The tallest of the peaks of the Bay Area at 4,343 feet, Mount St. Helena, an extinct volcano, was named for Russian princess Helena Garagin, who was one of the first to climb to its summit. Robert Louis Stevenson honeymooned here.

Calistoga area. In the museum store you can purchase books by and about Stevenson and pick up souvenirs of your visit.

Of course, the real attraction in Calistoga remains the hot springs and the mud baths that can be sampled at a number of places in town. A treatment in the warm mud, which reaches temperatures of 90° to 100°, is akin to a religious experience. Adventurous souls who are so inclined are immersed in a combination of peat moss, volcanic ash, and clay that has been mixed with hot water from the local geothermal springs. The

Up, Up and Away.
Soaring high above the verdant vine-yards in a hot-air balloon lends another perspective to exploration of the historic Napa Valley region.

Joseph Woods

water lends the mixture a slightly sulfurous smell that is quickly over-come by the application of wintergreen-scented washcloths applied to the bather's head. After several minutes in the relaxing mud, you arise on wobbly legs to rinse off in a warm shower, followed by another relaxing turn in a whirlpool. The whole process is undeniably refreshing, but tends to put one in the mood for a nap before embarking on any further explorations of the valley.

Speaking of that — exploration, not the nap — while you're in Calis-toga you might want to take advantage of an aerial tour of the valley by booking a sailplane ride at the Calistoga center. Alternative aerial views of the valley are offered by hot-air balloon operations in Napa and Yountville.

Oakville Grocery.
Be it for gourmet delicacies or the basics for a wine-and-cheese picnic, the well-stocked Oakville Grocery is a must stop for visitors to the Wine Country.

End of a Perfect Tour.
Sampling the superb fare in one of the valley's many excellent restaurants is an ideal way to end your visit to the Napa Valley Wine Country.

Joseph Woods

While I limited my formal tours to just three wineries, it must be noted that I did take the time to partake of a Napa Valley tradition — the wine-and-cheese picnic. It's said that the French have raised a bottle of wine, a baguette, and cheese to the level of high-art picnicking; however I think even they could learn something from the practitioners here.

Eating Out

Taking a cue from other travelers, after leaving Calistoga I backtracked to Oakville and the Oakville Grocery where I picked up the essentials to accompany the wine purchased during my tours. An establishment that is a yuppie's dream, this store specializes in outfitting picnickers with exotic supplies and gourmet items. Besides a wide variety of baskets and a complete selection of wines representing the valley's vintners, the grocery offers such things as duck volaille paté, smoked salmon, truffles, gourmet mustards and cheeses, and a good selection of fresh fruit. Once you've gathered these items, ask the folks at Oakville for directions to the local picnic areas, or consult the material you picked up in Napa for sites. Above all, you must make it a full-blown picnic.

While you're enjoying the picnic, however, remember to leave some room to accommodate a dinner at one of the valley's renowned restaurants. Exceptionally fine restaurants can be found in just about any of the small communities you'll pass through in Napa Valley, and I would heartily recommend you ignore the expense and treat yourself to a meal at one of these highly rated establishments. Two things to bear in mind: Don't be put off by the exterior appearance of the restaurant (some of the best places in the valley have a rather plain face); remember that most of the restaurants are small and very popular, making reservations a must.

POINTS OF INTEREST: California Tour 4

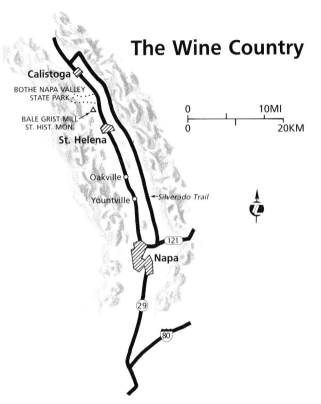

The Wine Country

Joseph Woods

ACCESS: From I-80, north on SR 29.

INFORMATION: *Napa Chamber of Commerce,* 1556 First Street, Napa, California 94559, (707) 226-7455; *St. Helena Chamber of Commerce,* 1080 Main Street, St. Helena, California 94574, (707) 963-4456; *Calistoga Chamber of Commerce,* 1458-4 Lincoln Avenue, Calistoga, California 94515, (707) 942-6333.

ANNUAL EVENTS:
Calistoga: *Easter Egg Hunt,* April; *Napa County Fair, Silverado Parade,* July; *Christmas Bazaar,* December.

Napa: *Napa Valley Marathon,* March; *Chili Cook-off,* May; *Napa Valley Wine Festival,* November.

Oakville: *Winter Classical Concerts,* Robert Mondavi Winery, January; *Robert Mondavi Winery Jazz Festival,* June.

Yountville: *Domaine Chandon Winery Fashion Show,* August; *Yountville Days Festival,* October.

MUSEUMS:
Calistoga: *Sharpsteen Museum,* 1311 Washington Street, (707) 942-5911. Daily, year-round.

St. Helena: *Silverado Museum,* off East Adams Street on Library Lane, (707) 963-3757, free, Tuesday–Sunday, year-round, noon–4.

SPECIAL ATTRACTIONS:
Calistoga: *Old Faithful Geyser of California,* north of town on Tubbs Lane Road, between SR 29 and SR 128, (707) 942-6463, daily, year-round; *Petrified Forest,* five miles west on Petrified Forest Road, (707) 942-6667, daily, year-round.

St. Helena: *Bale Grist Mill State Historical Park,* three miles northwest of town on SR 29, (707) 942-4575, daily, year-round, except holidays.

OUTFITTERS:
Calistoga: *Calistoga Soaring Center,* 1546 Lincoln Avenue, Calistoga, California 94515, (707) 942-5592, *Once In A Lifetime Balloon Company,* 1458 Lincoln Avenue, #12, Calistoga, California 94515, (707) 942-6541.

Napa: *Balloon Aviation of Napa Valley,* 2299 Third Street, Napa, California 94559, (707) 252-7067.

Yountville: *Napa Valley Balloons Inc.,* P.O. Box 2860, Yountville, California 94599, (707) 253-2224.

RESTAURANTS AND WINERIES: Both restaurants and wineries are too numerous to list here. Obtain winery tour schedules and restaurant listings from chambers of commerce listed above, or from other local outlets.

San Francisco to Point Reyes

*A city born overnight that has lived a
thousand years in a hundred.*

Herb Caen, *San Francisco Chronicle*

Michele Burgess

Much has been said and written about San Francisco, a lot of it contradictory, and all of it true. While some people come to this city for its trendiness, excitement, and the artful tawdriness of North Beach and the Tenderloin, others come to soak up its sophistication or to be charmed by Chinatown, the cable cars, and the beauty of its fog-shrouded bay. As for me, I keep coming back because, as the novelist Brian Moore notes, "San Francisco remains for me the ultimate romantic, faraway place."

RVing by the Bay

If San Francisco is all of these things, however, I have to admit one thing: What it isn't is an inviting place to drive an RV. The sheer volume of traffic, the steep hills, and the maze of streets make it both harrowing and nerve racking to try to maneuver a motorhome or trailer through San Francisco for any appreciable distance. Happily, that isn't necessary because San Francisco is one of the few U.S. cities that boasts a full-service RV park within its limits.

A City RV Park

The folks at San Francisco RV Park say they offer RVers a "front row center" view of the city, and that is a fairly accurate characterization. Located on King Street, in an area south of Market Street, this park is the ideal base from which to launch your forays into the city. Although there have been persistent rumors that this park could become a victim of the urban renewal that is sweeping through this area, I am happy to say that the management reports their lease was renewed in late 1987 for another five years.

That's the good news. The bad news is that there is a premium price to be paid for the convenience of parking your rig in the city. But before you object too strongly to the average overnight rate that is crowding $30, consider the fact that accommodations anywhere in San Francisco go for top dollar. (Tony Bennett may have left his heart here, but you can bet he also left a little cash.) You'll count your blessings when you learn that the average price of a hotel room in the City by the Bay is well over $100. If you still think the rate is too steep, however, there are alternatives south, down the peninsula or north, across the Golden Gate Bridge.

No matter where you stay, before you head into "The City" (as the natives call it), remember that you are probably going to do a lot of walking, much of which will be up and down San Francisco's famous hills. Comfortable shoes are a must. Also, while the city has a fairly mild year-round climate, the weather in San Francisco can be unpredictable and tends toward the damp. You can start out in bright sunshine in

Tour **5** *45 miles*

SAN FRANCISCO • SAUSALITO • MILL VALLEY • MOUNT TAMALPAIS • MUIR WOODS NATIONAL MONUMENT • BOLINAS LAGOON • POINT REYES STATION • POINT REYES NATIONAL SEASHORE

Painted Ladies.
Rainbow-hued detached rowhouses (circa 1895), built in Queen-Anne style by Matthew Kavanaugh, contrast against the modern skyline of San Francisco.

Night-time Sparkle.
The sparkling outline of San Francisco's night-time skyline can be mistaken for that of no other city in the world.

Michele Burgess

August, with temperatures in the high seventies, and by mid-afternoon find yourself walking through the heavy mist of a fog rolling in off the bay. Or, you can encounter gray skies and ocean-grown gales that take the wind-chill factor down to frigid winter temperatures.

Sightseeing by Bus, Cable Car and Foot

If you elect to stay at the San Francisco RV Park, grab a MUNI (municipal transportation) schedule in the campground office and catch the bus right behind the park, at Fourth and Townsend. From this point, take the bus that stops at Third and Market streets, since that drops you within a few blocks of the cable cars at Powell and Ellis. It also gives you a good starting point for browsing through the shops and stores in the heart of the downtown area. If you want to save your downtown excursions for later, the buses outside the park will also take you to Chinatown, North Beach, Fisherman's Wharf, Ghirardelli Square, and the fascinating Maritime Museum, Fort Mason, or the Palace of Fine Arts. If you're unsure of which bus to take, ask the driver for help. Some have the temperaments of New York cab drivers, but most are more than willing to steer tourists in the right direction.

When you board the bus, be sure to ask the driver for a transfer. Transfers are good for two hours, but each time you use one to board another bus, you get another transfer that is good for two more hours. Thus, those who are adept at translating the bus schedule to their chosen destinations in San Francisco's varied geography can tour the entire city for a small initial investment. In fact I learned the transfer trick from a silver-haired RVer I met at the bus stop. With great delight he told me how, using transfers and his senior citizen discount, he and his wife had covered nearly the entire city the day before at a cost of a mere twenty-five cents each.

Besides the obvious appeal to the parsimonious, I found the bus could also be an entertaining form of transportation. Shortly after I boarded one morning, the driver pulled to the curb a few blocks up the route to pick up a passenger dressed in a full gorilla suit that was topped off with a high school letterman's jacket. The gorilla paid his fare, dutifully tucked his transfer into his pocket, then proceeded to shuffle up and down, grunting and generally doing a fairly credible imitation of a member of the great ape family. As the driver continued unflinchingly along his route, the gorilla's antics quickly separated the bus passengers into two distinct groups. While the blasé, sophisticated natives barely glanced up from their morning papers, the wide-eyed tourists looked on first with alarm, then amusement, as the shaggy beast cavorted in the aisle.

Finally, three blocks later, the show ended as quickly as it began when the gorilla paused long enough to pull the cord to signal his stop, alighted, and went shuffling down the street. The baffling thing is the fellow in the gorilla suit did not appear to be one of San Francisco's countless street entertainers. He never passed the hat; his sole motivation seemed to be the joy of entertaining early-morning commuters.

While a bus ride in San Francisco can offer elements of the theater of the absurd, the city itself is a vast stage where aspiring musicians, jugglers, and mimes seem to populate every street corner, and where other entertainments can be found just in browsing the city's many distinct neighborhoods.

Leaving the bus at Third and Market streets gives you an ideal starting point for exploring the city. You can hop a cable car at Powell and Ellis and head north up Powell, going all the way to the bay and Hyde Street Pier and Fisherman's Wharf. Or you can make stops in between to visit shops along the way. Bear in mind, however, that contrary to popular belief, the colorful cable cars travel a confined route, and thus offer very limited access to the city.

An alternative I found enjoyable was to strike out on foot up Powell to Union Square, a picturesque opening in a canyon of high-rise buildings that make up the central section of the city. In San Francisco's early days this square was, in fact, the geographical center of the city and a popular gathering place for its residents. It takes its name from the Civil War era when the citizens of San Francisco held meetings here to demonstrate solidarity for the Union.

Today, because it is within easy walking distance of many of the hotels and commercial buildings in the downtown area, Union Square has become a popular gathering place or rest stop for tourists, brown baggers, and hordes of pigeons. In the mid-afternoon, when the sun is overhead and the crowds — but not the ubiquitous pigeons — have thinned, the square can be an island of tranquility where one can pause to rest and soak up the unique atmosphere of the city.

From the square it is just a short walk to some of the city's most elegant shops and stores along Post, Geary, Kearny and Stockton streets and Grant Avenue. Here you'll find Macy's, Neiman-Marcus, Saks Fifth Ave-

Audrey Gibson

Colorful Conveyance.
Part of an excellent mass transit system, the famed cable cars are the most colorful way to travel from the city to the sea.

City Oasis.
An island of green in the midst of a bustling city, historic Union Square is a perfect stop for foot-weary travelers.

nue, and Tiffany's, as well as local institutions such as Cable Car Clothiers and Bullock & Jones, purveyors of traditional men's clothing since 1853.

Up to Chinatown

For shopping with an international flavor, a walk up (up is the operative word here) Grant Avenue takes you to the Chinatown gateway at Grant and Bush, where the ornate green and red gate welcomes visitors into what is truly another world. Walking up along narrow, crowded Grant Avenue the first impression may be that one has wandered into a Hollywood re-creation of a street in Hong Kong or Shanghai. Bear in mind that Grant is the street that attracts the most tourist traffic in Chinatown; therefore, it tends to be the face it presents to the outside world. The numerous trinket shops found along this thoroughfare can quickly give one the impression that Chinatown is one big tourist trap. But wander into some of the side streets where you'll encounter more authentic examples of Chinese culture, and you'll swear you have been transported to the Far East.

Take a walk down Waverly Place, a street lined with Buddhist temples, or stroll narrow Spofford Street and stop in at one of the herb-and-tea shops. Besides the usual tourist paraphernalia and souvenirs, careful shoppers can find high-quality fabrics, rugs, dinnerware, and furniture along Grant, Stockton, and the intersecting side streets. For instance, I found that Tai Nam Yang on Grant had an excellent selection of porcelain vases at prices ranging from about $50 all the way up to $300. For colorful cloisonné enamel work, try the Canton Bazaar, also on Grant.

Faces of Another World.
Traditional Chinese masks peer back at visitors to San Francisco's world-renowned Chinatown. Walking its streets is a visit to another culture.

Gateway to the Far East.
Pass through the Grant Avenue gate to Chinatown and enter a new world of tea rooms, shops, temples, and ancient and modern Chinese culture.

If at all possible, time your visit to Chinatown to coincide with the lunch or dinner hour so you can sample some authentic Chinese cuisine. Johnny Kan's and The Empress of China on Grant are perhaps the best-known restaurants, but numerous other eating establishments are scattered throughout Chinatown. I dropped in at the Asia Garden on Pacific Avenue to sample some of the legendary dim sum (Chinese tea cakes); they did not disappoint. Some other good bets are Tung Fong and the Hong Kong Tea House, also on Pacific, or Sam Wo's on Grant.

For RVers who might want to re-create authentic Chinese dishes in their rig's galley, the place to go for ingredients is the May Wah Trading Company or the Mandarin Delight, both on Stockton Street. For genuine Chinese cooking utensils, try Ginn Wall Hardware on Grant Avenue, or the Ying Company on Stockton Street. At both shops you will find a full range of bamboo steamers, woks, Mongolian hot pots, and myriad other essentials.

To top off your walking tour of Chinatown, stop by the Chinese Cultural Center in the Holiday Inn on Kearny Street. The guided tours and art displays at the center are a good way to delve a little more deeply into the Chinese culture and come away with a better understanding of the life-styles of those who populate the sixteen-square-block area known as Chinatown.

Echoes of the Orient.
From intricate lamp posts to colorfully capped roofs, the ornate architecture of San Francisco's Chinatown remains faithful to its Far East origins.

Down to Fisherman's Wharf

From the heart of Chinatown, a two-block walk west from Grant Avenue takes you back to Powell Street, where you can hop a cable car for the short ride down to Fisherman's Wharf. The folks at the San Francisco

Square-Rigged Beauty.
Launched in 1886, the historic *Balclutha* is now permanently berthed at Pier 43, where it hosts visitors to the National Maritime Museum.

Chamber of Commerce told me that they estimate that more than eighty percent of the visitors who come to the city flock to this region to soak up the colorful atmosphere of the fishing boats, maritime history, and restaurants. With that many tourists descending on one area of the city each year, it's no wonder that Fisherman's Wharf has earned the reputation (well deserved) of late of being a tourist trap.

Despite the fact that you'll find some shops here that sell all manner of overpriced junk, this area is still worth a stop for a number of reasons. First, there is the Cannery, a converted peach cannery that now houses some excellent art galleries, shops, and a market that offers a variety of tasty delicacies, including rich chocolates and mouth-watering pastries. A few blocks west, fronting Beach Street and across from Aquatic Park, there is Ghirardelli Square, a converted Civil-War-era woolen mill that was used for a time as a chocolate factory and now houses retail shops, bookstores, bars, and restaurants.

For history buffs there are the fascinating National Maritime Museum and the old ships berthed at Hyde Street Pier. The West Coast's largest maritime museum, this National Park Service facility features ship models, artifacts, and photographs that take visitors back to the days of the gold rush, Cape Horners, and early fishing vessels that worked the San Francisco Bay and northern California coastline. At the pier you can board and explore three well-preserved, historic ships: the *Eureka,* a double-ended, walking beam ferryboat; the *C.A. Thayer,* a sailing schooner circa 1895; and the *Wapama,* a steam schooner built in 1915 to haul lumber and other cargo.

The centerpiece of the historic ship exhibit here is the *Balclutha,* a square-rigged, Cape Horn sailing ship, launched in 1886, that carried wine, whiskey, wool, rice, and coal. At the time of my visit the *Balclutha* was still undergoing restoration, but a helpful and informative ranger told me the ship would also be open for first-hand exploration once work was completed. Besides the ship tours, there are two other ships — the *Alma* and the *Hercules* — that can be viewed from the pier, as well as an audio program that takes you on a self-guided tour, a film that depicts the last voyage of the *Thayer,* and weekend programs that include demonstrations of nautical skills and lectures on sea lore.

Street Scenes

From the museum or the pier it's an easy walk to Aquatic Park, a good place to pause, catch your breath, and take in some of the local color of the wharf area. In addition to the joggers and tourists that come here, the park is also a favorite site for street entertainers. At various times of the day you are likely to find guitarists, jugglers, saxophonists, mimes, and other performers who demonstrate their respective talents in return for "donations" from their audience. Some are quite good, and dropping a little something in the hat is a way of contributing to a long-standing San Francisco tradition. After a respite at Aquatic Park, consider strolling down the Golden Gate Promenade, a 3½-mile scenic walk that follows the shoreline from the park to Fort Point National Historic Site under the Golden Gate Bridge.

Of course, no visit to Fisherman's Wharf would be complete without taking the time to sample some of the excellent fresh seafood served at famous restaurants such as Sabella's, Tarentino's, and Alioto's. For those who just want a quick snack, fresh crab and shrimp cocktails can be purchased from streetside vendors. You should also come away with a fresh loaf of the famous San Francisco sourdough bread; take it back to your rig and enjoy it with sweet butter and a bottle of California wine.

Out in the bay is one of the city's most famous (or infamous) sites, Alcatraz Island, a bleak, rock-strewn outcropping upon which rests the gray walls of a federal penitentiary that was once home to some of the nation's most notorious criminals, including Al Capone; Robert Stroud, the Birdman of Alcatraz; and Machine Gun Kelly. Tours of the facility are offered daily, year-round, by National Park Service rangers. There is also a self-guided cell block tour that offers opportunities to get pictures of yourself "in stir." Round-trip boat tickets for the visit to Alcatraz can be purchased at Pier 41 on Fisherman's Wharf.

Michele Burgess

A Walk on the Town.
Ghirardelli Square (above) is a popular gathering place for locals and tourists to shop, eat, and people-watch. Street entertainers like the minstrel (below) make an adventure out of an afternoon on the town.

Michele Burgess

Palace of Fine Arts.
A science museum is housed inside the graceful Palace of Fine Arts, set in a park with a lagoon where swans and ducks glide by.

About two miles west of Fisherman's Wharf, off Marina Boulevard, is the Palace of Fine Arts. Built for the Panama-Pacific Exhibition of 1915, the Palace was constructed of plaster of Paris and was not intended to remain as a permanent structure. When the Palace refused to crumble, San Francisco assured its place as a permanent part of the landscape with a major renovation project in 1967. Today the Palace, standing majestically above a blue reflecting pool, houses a museum of 500 scientific exhibits.

The Gift of Golden Gate Park

On the west side of the San Francisco peninsula, Golden Gate Park is another must-stop for RVers who have the time. One of the great city parks of the world, visitors here will be hard pressed to imagine that the 1,017 acres of lush greenery were cultivated from sand dunes made barren by the unceasing winds off the Pacific Ocean. Though the land was acquired in 1870 and a basic design for the park was laid out in 1871 by William Hammond Hall, a civil engineer, it took vision and plain hard work to mold the land to what it is today.

The credit goes to one man, John McLaren, a stubborn Scottish landscape architect who dreamed and developed the park over a period of fifty-five years. McLaren's reputation for making things grow was legendary, and he lived up to that reputation by turning the desolate region into a grassy and wooded wonderland. On his ninety-third birthday McLaren was still at it when the city fathers decided to reward him for his efforts. When asked what he wanted most of all, McLaren quickly replied, "More manure for me trees."

While McLaren was passionate about his trees, he was just as strongly opposed to his park being populated with statues to honor fallen heroes and civic leaders. When statues were erected, over his objections, he solved the problem by encircling them with new trees and shrubbery until they were eventually lost in the overgrowth. The great irony is that a statue of the diminutive McLaren now graces the entrance to his beloved rhododendron dell.

For me, the highlights of the park are the Strybing Arboretum and Botanical Gardens and the Conservatory of Flowers. The seventy-acre arboretum boasts a collection of more than 5,000 species of plants and includes the Demonstration Garden and the Garden of Fragrance for the visually impaired. The elegant, glistening conservatory, located off John F. Kennedy Drive, just inside the park entrance off Stanyan Street, has been modeled after the Palm House in London's famed Kew Gardens. Built in 1878 in Dublin, it was shipped around Cape Horn in sections to be reassembled at the present site in the park. The conservatory now stands as the oldest structure in the park — a grand survivor of the devastating 1906 earthquake — sheltering within its walls brilliant displays of delicate tropical plants. Of special interest is a mist-making machine added recently which periodically bathes both plants and visitors in a warm, dense fog.

Besides its beautiful foliage, Golden Gate Park now offers a number of attractions, including the California Academy of Sciences, Morrison Planetarium, Steinhart Aquarium, the Asian Art Museum, Conservatory of Flowers, Children's Playground (with restored equipment dating back to the turn of the century), and a Japanese tea garden where weary visitors can pause for a refreshing cup of hot tea accompanied by fortune cookies and oriental pastries. The park is also home to the San Francisco Mime Troupe, an activist theater group that presents skits and plays.

Not far from the park (north on Stanyon Street, west on Tuck Street to Van Ness, then south two blocks), I found the civic center buildings at Van Ness and McAllister worth a stop just to view the ornate, gold-encrusted city hall building. Built in 1914, this structure boasts a dome taller than the U.S. Capitol, and features a massive interior hall with a magnificent stairway that climbs to the second-floor board of supervisors' chamber. Also located in this complex of buildings are the San Francisco Museum of Art and the city's famed opera house.

Michele Burgess

Michele Burgess

Let Me Entertain You.
Artists and musicians are prevalent on the streets of San Francisco and add a unique charm to "The City."

Michele Burgess

The Old and the New.
"The City" prides itself on both the preservation of its traditional heritage and its openness to innovation and growth, creating an interesting juxtaposition of architecture.

At last the mighty task is done;
Resplendent in the western sun
The bridge looms mountain high;
Its titan piers grip ocean floor,
Its great steel arms link shore
  with shore,
Its towers pierce the sky.
        Joseph E. Strauss

Shopping and Dining Opportunities

From here, serious shoppers — those who have world-class status — should continue south on Van Ness and take Market Street east to the Embarcadero Center in San Francisco's financial district. Here, bounded by Sacramento, Clay, Battery, and Drumm streets, there is a four-tower high-rise complex that houses countless shops, restaurants, and galleries. It is a universe unto itself where, if not careful, you can lose yourself in an orgy of spending that is not likely to stop until you top out on your credit limit or your card melts.

If all this has left you a little weary, grab a few winks in your rig before planning a night on the town at one of San Francisco's first-rate restaurants. It has been estimated that the city has more than 4,300 dining establishments that qualify as full-service restaurants. One look at the restaurant listings in the phone directory will confirm that figure can't be far from wrong. The offerings here run the gamut from nouvelle California cuisine and some of the country's most superb ethnic eateries, to good old American meat and potatoes. When you're selecting a restaurant, bear in mind that San Franciscans approach dining as an art form. For that reason, most of the city's finer establishments require reservations and a coat and tie for admission.

After dinner, you'll find unlimited opportunities for entertainment into the wee hours of the morning. There are the San Francisco Ballet, Opera, and Symphony for the culturally inclined, and plenty of intimate clubs where one can hear excellent jazz bands or vocalists who specialize in the old standards. And for the adventurous there is the North Beach scene. Here energy and excitement abound along Broadway, a street that basks in the riotous, multi-colored glow of thousands of flashing lights, and echoes with the din of barkers who attempt to lure visitors into clubs that promise all manner of lurid entertainment.

If a night on the town leaves you rising a little late the next morning, you'll still have plenty of time to make your rig roadworthy for the short trip across the Golden Gate Bridge and into the backroads of Marin County and Point Reyes National Seashore.

Open Up Your Golden Gate

For those staying at the San Francisco RV Park, your route, and the best bet for escaping some of the city traffic, is to turn left out of the park entrance, go east to Third Street, turn north, and pick up I-80 heading west. Once on the interstate, continue west until you come to the transition with US 101, then head north on the short loop that deadends at Fulton. From there follow the signs that will direct you to US 101/Van Ness Avenue, or turn east on Fulton and then north on US 1/Park Presidio Drive. Both routes eventually link up with the toll plaza entrance to the Golden Gate Bridge, with the US 1 option probably being the best choice. (**Note:** No toll is charged for northbound traffic.)

A few driving tips for RVers are necessary at this point. Unfortunately for those heading north, there is no way to leave San Francisco without

California Office of Tourism

The Golden Gate Bridge.
As visitors leave San Francisco for Marin County, the city offers one of its most famous views as a good-bye gift.

utilizing the surface streets. While Van Ness and Park Presidio are both four-lane routes, they are often congested, and navigating through the traffic can be nerve racking since few motorists want to yield to RVers. Patience and plodding are the watchwords here. Your blood pressure will remain at normal levels if you sit back and make the best of it.

Similar advice holds for the crossing of the bridge itself. I found it best to stay in the inside lane while crossing the Golden Gate because the lanes are narrow and the outside lane tends to cut close to lamps and signposts. I have heard reports of RVers being crowded into the curb and damaging their rigs by clipping lights and signs.

Hunter S. Thompson said it best in his book, *A Generation of Swine*:

> Driving the bridge has never been safe, but in recent years — ever since it became a sort of low-tech Rube Goldberg experiment for traffic flow specialists — it has become a maze of ever-changing uncertain lanes and a truly fearful experience to drive. At least half the lanes are always blocked off by flashing lights, fireballs and huge generator trucks full of boiling asphalt and crews of wild-eyed men wearing hard hats and carrying picks and shovels.
>
> They are never gone, and the few lanes they leave open for what they call "civilian traffic" are often littered with huge red Lane Markers that look like heavy iron spittoons and cause terror in the heart of any unwitting driver who doesn't know they are rubber. . . . Nobody wants to run over one of those things, except on purpose, and in that case you want to take out a whole stretch of them, maybe 15 or 19 in a single crazed pass at top speed with the door hanging open.

Just over the bridge you can pause for a closer look at the Golden Gate Bridge at the Vista Point parking lot, which allows ample space for RVs. On those days when the fog is rolling in off the bay and intermittently covering the bridge and the San Francisco skyline, the changing panorama can provide an excellent opportunity for some terrific photos.

While the view from this vantage point can be truly breathtaking, the undeniable centerpiece is the Golden Gate Bridge itself. Alternately described in elaborate metaphors ("a golden necklace around the throat of San Francisco," or "a steel harp," the bridge is truly an engineering marvel. Appropriately, the bridge's golden anniversary was marked in 1987 with a year-long celebration that was highlighted by a three-day Bridge Fest in May.

The design and construction of the bridge was led by Joseph Baermann Strauss, a Chicago engineer, who drew up the first plans for the span in 1921 and then spent the next nine years trying to convince San Francisco's civic leaders that the bridge could be built at a reasonable cost. Actual construction began in January, 1933, and the bridge was completed and opened to traffic on May 28, 1937, at a total cost of more than $20 million.

Marin County

Just north of Vista Point is a turnoff to a road that drops steeply down to the main thoroughfare of Bridgeway in the tiny bayside village of Sausalito. The narrow road, combined with limited and strictly enforced parking, make this a less-than-inviting stop for drivers of large RVs. Still, if you can manage it, Sausalito (from the Spanish *saucelito* meaning "little willow") is worth a closer look, both for its splendid view of San Francisco and as an introduction to trendy Marin County.

Golden Gate Escape.
RVers exiting San Francisco for the hills of Marin County will find the drive across the Golden Gate bridge both scenic and challenging.

Michele Burgess

With a population of less than 8,000 crammed into a tiny area that hugs the steep bluffs here, Sausalito could almost be characterized as a community of modern cliff dwellers. If you can find a place to park your rig, take a walk down Bridgeway and browse through some of the galleries and craft shops. Drop into any of the restaurants along the main drag and you will be virtually assured of an excellent meal. If possible try to visit Sausalito during a weekday when the streets and shops are less crowded, and you'll have an opportunity to inspect the handmade jewelry, pottery, and other crafts in an unhurried atmosphere.

If you have the misfortune of getting entangled in heavy traffic in Sausalito, one consolation is that getting out of town is easier than getting in. Simply follow Bridgeway north past the rows of houseboats bobbing in the bay until it brings you back to US 101 at Marin City. One of the few bay area cities that is not oriented to tourist traffic, Marin City's only claim to fame is its flea market, which is open every weekend throughout the summer.

Almost as soon as you fall into the traffic flow on the main highway you'll come to the turnoff for SR 1, which cuts west toward the Pacific coastline. As this route begins to wind toward the ocean, the scenery becomes truly stunning, with excellent vistas of the lush, green rolling hills and seaside bluffs. Before reaching the ocean, however, you'll want to take the little road that winds around the base of Mount Tamalpais to the community of Mill Valley.

California Office of Tourism

Mount "Tam."
Mount Tamalpais, called the "Sleeping Maiden" for its gentle contours, offers some thirty miles of trails. Hikers will be rewarded by magnificent Pacific views.

Majestic Giants.
Walled in by majestic coast redwoods, the deeply shaded trails of the Muir Woods National Monument lead through lush woodlands where the silence is broken only by calling birds and a babbling brook.

At this point take a deep breath because you're about to enter the capital of California's hot-tub culture and an area that contains some of the most expensive real estate in the country. Nestled at the base of Mount Tamalpais (Mt. Tam as the locals call it), Mill Valley is a community that is blessed with Old World charm and a stunning natural setting that is unequaled anywhere in the world. Unfortunately, in the last decade the community has become better known for its upscale residents who have flocked here "to find themselves" through all manner of quirky cults and mystical therapies.

Take time to explore the town's shops and galleries or pick up some tasty, freshly baked pastries and breads at the bakeries along Throckmorton Avenue. My favorite spot here is the Book Depot, a renovated railway station that contains an excellent sampling of literature, ranging from the lastest bestsellers and classics to more obscure works by local poets and writers. RVers who like to get into the backcountry will also like the Book Depot for its selection of local hiking maps.

Some of the best of those trails are to be found on the slopes of Mt. Tam, also dubbed the "Sleeping Maiden" by residents because of the voluptuous bumps and curves of her ridgeline. Within a space of 6,000 acres, hikers are offered some thirty miles of trails. Those who trudge through the intermittent fog to break out in the sunshine of Mt. Tam's peak will be rewarded with a magnificent view of the Pacific.

Into the (Muir) Woods

Before driving the final leg to the ocean, RVers will want to make one more stop at Muir Woods National Monument, a lush, dense stand of redwoods clustered at the base of Mount Tamalpais. While these famed woods bear the name of John Muir, they owe their existence to a wealthy Marin native, William Kent, who purchased the land and then deeded it to the federal government so the great redwoods would be forever protected. Although Theodore Roosevelt asked that the woods be named after Kent, the offer was graciously declined, and Kent asked instead that they be named after naturalist John Muir.

Anyone who takes the time to stop by the woods today will be immediately taken by the ghostly quiet that pervades the area, giving it an almost hallowed atmosphere. That serenity has been assured by a restriction that limits all motorized vehicles to the broad, shaded parking lot. Those who want to get a closer look at the woods can do so by hiking the six miles of trails that wind through the giant trees. It's an easy walk and well worth the effort.

The Panoramic Highway

From Muir Woods an exceptionally scenic route, appropriately called the Panoramic Highway, winds along the ridges, in and out of the valleys, and eventually drops down to link up with SR 1. Despite the temptation of the scenery, however, I would not recommend this road for most RVs because it is just too narrow and winding. A better choice is to take the Muir Woods loop back to SR 1 and continue from there to Muir and Stinson beaches. These are extremely popular areas for surf fishing, but also draw a number of sunbathers on summer weekends. If you want to cast a line for surf perch or rockfish, Muir and Stinson are worth a stop.

If you are not an angler, an alternative is to continue the scenic drive up the coast and make your next stop the Bolinas Lagoon, a 1,000-acre nature preserve that attracts a wide variety of shorebirds and several species of ducks. At the nearby Audubon Canyon Ranch, a special observatory will allow you to view nesting herons and egrets.

Incidentally, at the end of the little spur road that leads to the lagoon, you'll find the small town of Bolinas. RVers who stop here run the risk of getting rebuffed by some of the community's decidedly unfriendly residents. A recent *San Francisco Chronicle* report noted that citizens of Bolinas are so xenophobic that they have taken to "misdirecting tourists, ripping out road signs, setting up blockades, trashing travel writers' vehicles (I emerged unscathed), smashing the windows of real estate offices and water-ballooning Winnebagos. . . ." This growing inhospitable reputation prompted columnist Herb Caen to call Bolinas "elitist, snobbish, ingrown, unfriendly, and not the world's greatest place for food." Enough said.

Entry to Point Reyes

From the lagoon, about twenty miles of fairly level and straight road will take you into the small town of Point Reyes Station, the official jumping-off point for entry into the peninsula of the Point Reyes National Seashore. In sharp contrast to those communities on the Marin headlands, Point Reyes Station has a rural, small-town atmosphere reminiscent of the midwest. With a population of about 1,000, the town offers a few of the obligatory arts-and-crafts shops, but there are also establishments like Toby's Feed Store that actually sells animal feed, saddles, and even a good selection of flea-and-tick spray. Down the street there is the Palace Market, displaying good produce and the catch of the day.

Turn off SR 1, continue to the seashore along Sir Frances Drake Boulevard, and, especially on summer weekends, you'll encounter a little more bustling atmosphere in the town of Inverness. To my mind a prime attraction here is the small, white cottage on Inverness Way, the home of Shaker Shops West, which sells fine reproductions of Shaker furniture, baskets, boxes, and utensils. Most of the items can be purchased complete or in kit form at fairly reasonable prices. The folks at the shop will be glad to arrange shipping back home if you don't have room in your rig.

Leaving Inverness, follow the Sir Frances Drake Highway as it dips and rises over the open slopes of Point Reyes. Named *La Punta de los Reyes* (the Point of Kings) by a Spanish sailor who was shipwrecked here in

Beach Walking.
Interesting patterns drawn on the water and the sand by the rhythmic movements of the wind create a living canvas to walk upon.

Jim Elder

Spectacular Sunset.
The unpredictable weather has a silver lining—clouds reflect against the sun and water to create breathtaking sunsets along the northern coast.

1603, Point Reyes has to be one of the most hauntingly beautiful regions along the California coast. This narrow spit of land jutting out into the Pacific also offers visitors an opportunity to explore some of this region's earliest history through its rich and varied offerings.

Perhaps the most logical place to start would be by backtracking about four miles south of Inverness to the park headquarters building on Bear Valley Road, where you can pick up a brochure and map of the park and a number of other pamphlets on the flora and fauna of the area. There is also an excellent selection for sale of more detailed books. Don't leave without taking the time to walk through the exceptionally lifelike exhibits in the natural history museum. For children there is a wonderful nature interpretive center.

Near the barnlike headquarters building, about a half-mile walk down a well-marked trail, stands Kule Loklo, a reconstructed Miwok Indian village. Started in 1976 as a joint effort of the National Park Service and the Miwok Archaeological Preserve of Marin, this village re-creates the Miwok culture of 5,000 years ago. Included in the exhibits are bark-covered huts called *kotcas,* a granary where the Indians stored acorns, and arboreal sunshades that protected workers as they labored over baskets, arrowheads, and other tools essential to their existence. Of special interest is the *lamma,* or ceremonial dance house, with its four poles that are said to hold the spiritual power of the north, south, east, and west. A center pole was reputedly so sacred that only the leaders of the tribe were permitted to touch it.

Before leaving the headquarters area another nearby stop is the Morgan Horse Ranch where the National Park Service breeds and raises patrol horses used throughout their facilities in the west. The ranch is spotlessly maintained, and the sleek horses grazing and frolicking along the open slopes of the pasturelands are a sight to behold.

Drake's Beach

Once armed with the appropriate background material obtained at the headquarters building, I would suggest you drive back along Sir Francis Drake Highway to Drake's Beach (on Drake's Bay). From the large, open parking lot you can walk down to the beach and the site where Sir Francis Drake reportedly landed on June 17, 1579.

Legend has it — disputed by some — that Drake put in here to effect repairs to his storm-tossed ship, the *Golden Hind.* According to an account written by Francis Fletcher, Drake's chaplain, the captain found the harbor to his liking and is said to have dubbed the inlet "Nova Albion" because it reminded him of the shores of his native England.

Stop in at the visitor center located near the beach and pick up some of the literature that details the controversy that has arisen over the years regarding Drake's visit here. Included are claims that this was not the site of his landing at all; rather, some historians say, it was farther south somewhere in San Francisco Bay. Although that debate rages on and is not likely to be resolved anytime soon, one indisputable fact is that the

California Office of Tourism

Drake's Beach.
Legend has it that Sir Francis Drake put in here to repair his ship, the *Golden Hind,* but some historians disagree. Stop at the visitor center for information to decide for yourself.

Point Reyes Lighthouse.
Touring the lighthouse includes a visit to a museum housing the original light, shipwreck photos, and antiques along with the unequaled view.

broad, level beach is a very inviting place for a stroll. A pamphlet distributed at the center provides a guide to the various markers erected along the beach commemorating certain events of his landing. A clean, sheltered picnic area near the beach is an ideal spot for a leisurely, scenic lunch before resuming your explorations.

Lighthouse at the Point

From Drake's Beach my wanderings took me to the highway's end at the Point Reyes lighthouse. Erected in 1870 as a response to an alarming increase in shipwrecks along the coast here, the lighthouse is uniquely situated halfway down a cliff, close to the rocky beach. Placement of the light there made construction both difficult and expensive, but it was chosen as the only feasible location because other lights in the area were too often obscured by fog. The old lighthouse provides a fascinating tour, and I found viewing the complex mechanism and getting a first-hand glimpse of life on this damp, isolated point of land one of the highlights of my visit here.

A few words of warning: Getting to the lighthouse requires walking down a long flight of stairs that is equivalent to a ten-story building. The walk down is easy, but remember you have to come back up. Another problem that visitors may encounter is the high volume of traffic that invades this area during the spring whale migrations. The Park Service people told me that as many as 14,000 people have tried to crowd into the area on some weekends. During whale-watching season, inquire about traffic at the headquarters office before making the drive.

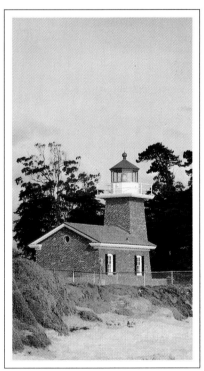

Leone Jones

Jim Elder

Point Reyes National Seashore.
Many species of birds and mammals live along the secluded beaches of Point Reyes National Seashore. Several tidepools offer a glimpse into the world below the shifting seas.

Trekking the Trails

Besides the windswept hills and beaches, a major attraction at Point Reyes is the excellent, 150-mile trail system that crisscrosses the area. While some of the pathways are steep and strenuous, many are fairly easy to walk. Three trails include backcountry camps for hikers. (Permits are required and can be obtained at the headquarters.) A prime motivation for getting out and hiking some of the trails, however, is that it is the only way you can get to see some of the best scenery the region has to offer. For instance, the Bear Valley Trail ends at Arch Rock and an open meadow that sits atop a fifty-foot cliff hovering over the Pacific. From there you can look down to be mesmerized by the awesome beauty of the waves crashing against the rock-strewn coastline.

A highly instructive walk is the Earthquake Trail, which takes visitors to the epicenter of the 1906 San Francisco earthquake. Included in the points of interest here is a fenceline that was shifted over fifteen feet by the earthquake. The trail covers just a little more than a half mile and has recently been paved by the Park Service so that it allows full access for wheelchairs. A favorite area of geologists, this definitely should be included in your Point Reyes meanderings.

POINTS OF INTEREST: California Tour 5

San Francisco to Pt. Reyes

[Map showing San Francisco to Pt. Reyes area with labels: Sir Francis Drake Hwy., Inverness, Pt. Reyes Station, Drake's Beach, Pt. Reyes Lighthouse, Drake's Bay, Point Reyes Nat'l Seashore, Panoramic Hwy., Muir Woods Nat'l Mon., Mt. Tamalpais, Bolinas, Bolinas Lagoon, Stinson Beach, Muir Beach, Golden Gate Bridge, Sausalito, Marin City, Oakland, San Francisco Bay, San Francisco, Pacific Ocean; scale 0-10MI, 0-20KM]

ACCESS: From the south, *US 101* to San Francisco; from the north *US 1*, south to *US 101.*

INFORMATION: *San Francisco Visitor Information Center,* Powell and Market streets, San Francisco, California 94103, (415) 974-6900; *Redwood Empire Association,* One Market Plaza, San Francisco, California 94105, (415) 543-8334; *MUNI* information, (415) 673-6864; *Point Reyes National Seashore,* Point Reyes, California 94956, (415) 663-1092.

ANNUAL EVENTS:
Novato: *Renaissance Pleasure Faire,* August.

San Francisco: *Fiddler's Contest,* January; *Sports and Boat Show,* January; *Chinese New Year,* February; *Daffodil Festival,* March; *Cherry Blossom Festival,* April; *Bay-to-Breakers Race,* May; *Rose Show,* May; *Gay Freedom Day Parade,* June; *San Francisco Fair and Exposition,* July; *San Francisco Opera Opening,* September; *Dickens Christmas Fair,*

November; *San Francisco Ballet, Nutcracker Suite,* December.

San Rafael: *Marin County Fair,* July.

MUSEUMS AND GALLERIES:
Novato: *Marin Museum of the American Indian,* 2200 Novato Boulevard, Tuesday–Sunday, year-round, (415) 897-4064.

San Francisco: *Academy of Sciences,* on Kennedy Drive in Golden Gate Park, daily, year-round, (415) 750-7145; *M. H. de Young Memorial Museum,* Kennedy Drive in Golden Gate Park, open Wednesday–Sunday, year-round, (415) 750-3659; *Museum of Modern Art,* Van Ness and McCallister streets, Tuesday–Sunday, year-round, (415) 556-8177; *Old U.S. Mint,* Fifth and Mission streets, Monday–Friday, year-round, except for major holidays, (415) 974-0788.

Sausalito: *Bay Model Visitor Center,* 2100 Bridgeway, Tuesday–Sunday during summer, Monday–Saturday, remainder of year, (415) 332-3870.

SPECIAL ATTRACTIONS:
Marin County: *Mount Tamalpais State Park,* six miles west of Mill Valley, (415) 388-2070, daily, year-round; *Muir Woods National Monument,* off SR 1 near Mill Valley, daily, year-round, (415) 388-2595.

San Francisco: *Alcatraz Island,* in San Francisco Bay, depart Pier 41 at Fisherman's Wharf, daily, year-round, (415) 546-2805.

RESTAURANTS:
Mill Valley: *The Buckeye Restaurant,* Highway 101, (415) 332-1292, German-American.

San Francisco: Renowned for the quality and variety of its dining experience, San Francisco has too many fine restaurants to list here. Obtain a list of restaurants from campground office or from one of the tourist information centers.

Sausalito: *Yet Wah Restaurant,* 300 Turney Street, (415) 331-3300, Chinese, family dining at reasonable prices.

HARTE, TWAIN, AND GOLD-RUSH MEMORIES
The Southern Mother Lode

I reached my hand down and picked it up; it made my heart thump, for I was certain it was gold.

James Marshall

Thomas Le Rose

Most visitors to the state think that California's Gold Country consists only of the John Sutter's Mill area in Coloma, site of the first major strike that started the gold rush of 1849. In fact, California's Mother Lode country stretches for nearly 200 miles, following the general path of historic SR 49 as it winds along the western slopes of the majestic Sierra Nevada mountain range.

Mountain Hideaways

Although the site of that first gold strike remains a fascinating place to visit, to my mind the best backroading experiences in the Mother Lode are the mountain hideaways and pristine river canyons at the north end of SR 49 (Tour 3) and the bucolic Sierra foothills of the region that was once called the Southern Mines. Here amid rolling pasturelands and green mountain slopes, RVers can find some of the best-preserved reminders of California's rip-roarin' gold rush.

Mariposa

Because of its easy access from SR 99, via SR 140, the Sierra foothill town of Mariposa (Spanish for "butterfly") is a good place to start a tour of the southern Mother Lode. With a strategic location at the junction of the main artery to Yosemite National Park and SR 49, this community of 1,200 gains its livelihood from tourism and, therefore, is especially hospitable to travelers.

Like a lot of towns in the Mother Lode, Mariposa (originally named Logtown because of its early timber industry) was the site of a major gold discovery in 1849. Thanks to that gold strike and the sometimes wily manipulation of Colonel John C. Fremont, the famed explorer, Mariposa grew rapidly to a position of prominence as the county seat. By 1854, during the heyday of the Mother Lode, Mariposa had grown to a population of several thousand and boasted one of the stateliest county courthouses in all of California. Unfortunately, after the mines began to play out, and after a disastrous fire swept through the town in 1860, many of Mariposa's residents drifted away.

Having survived its earlier misfortunes, Mariposa's citizens now have preserved some of the relics of its glory days. The white-frame courthouse with its magnificent clock tower stands lovingly preserved at the north end of town, one block east of SR 299. It now has the distinction of being the oldest county courthouse in continuous operation in California. Other points of interest here include St. Joseph's Catholic Church, built in 1862 atop a bluff at the south edge of town; the Old Jail, on Bullion Street, built in 1858 and fully restored just a few years ago; the Trabucco-Campbell home on Jones Street, a magnificent Victorian built in 1901;

Tour 6 *75 miles*
Side trip to Calaveras Big Trees, 25 miles

MARIPOSA • MT. BULLION • HORNITOS • BEAR VALLEY • COULTERVILLE • CHINESE CAMP • JAMESTOWN • SONORA • COLUMBIA STATE HISTORIC PARK • JACKASS HILL • MARK TWAIN CABIN • STANISLAUS RIVER • CARSON HILL • ANGELS CAMP • CALAVERAS BIG TREES STATE PARK •

Backroad Barn.
Bucolic views, such as this weathered old barn standing sentinel in the Sierra foothills of California's Gold Country, await the backroad traveler on SR 49.

and, nearby on the corner of Jones Street, the former office of the *Mariposa Gazette,* which now houses the local chamber of commerce.

For me, the highlight of my stop here was the Mariposa County Museum and History Center at 12th and Jessie streets. You'll find a remarkably complete collection of artifacts from the gold-rush era at this facility, including re-creations of living quarters used by miners, an Indian village, and a number of carriages and other horse-drawn vehicles. Without a doubt, the outstanding exhibit is a completely restored mill (used to extract gold from rocks) located on the museum grounds.

Rolling north from town, SR 49 crosses Mariposa Creek and passes through Mt. Bullion, a tiny community that was the site of the Princeton Mine, which yielded $3 million in gold in the 1850s. For those who have the time, I recommend a side trip by turning south on the road just north of Mt. Bullion and driving thirteen miles to the historic town of Hornitos.

Hornitos

This sleepy hamlet was once one of the rowdiest towns in the entire Mother Lode. Murders and other crimes were common, prompting one street to be named Dead Man's Alley and a nearby ravine to be dubbed Dead Man's Gulch. With a population of less than 150, Hornitos is now much more sedate and is notable primarily for its picturesque setting, ruins, and historic relics that include an old jail, the Hornitos School, built in 1860, and the remains of one of the first general stores operated by San Francisco's D. Ghirardelli & Company.

From Hornitos I found the easiest way to return to SR 49 is to take the narrow, winding CR 116 that in eleven miles joins the highway at the village of Bear Valley. Again, just a skeleton of its former self, Bear Valley's few remaining structures are all that are left of a once-thriving community of 3,000 that died with the gold rush. Beside the highway are the ruins of the once rowdy Bon Ton Saloon, an old jail, and crumbling schoolhouse. A well-equipped general store and gas station are the only businesses left in town today.

From Hornitos, SR 49 leaves the wide open spaces of Bear Valley and hugs the Sierra foothills as it snakes its way northward. Prepare for slow going as the highway begins its steep descent into the scenic Merced River Canyon before climbing back out of the gorge and winding on to the town of Coulterville. Although the route from Bear Valley to Coulterville is less than thirty miles, I found that it took nearly an hour.

Coulterville

As luck would have it, I rolled into Coulterville the weekend that the town was kicking off its First Annual Gold Rush Days celebration. After finding a suitable spot to park my motorhome, I strolled back to the center of town and rounded the corner on Main Street just in time to walk into the midst of a staged bank robbery. With the sheriff and his deputies in hot pursuit, the desperadoes were captured before they could get very far with their ill-gotten gains, but not, however, before

Desperadoes.
Coulterville's rowdy days as a wide-open gold-rush town come to life each year in an annual Old West celebration.

Sierra Foothills.
Following SR 49's winding route
through the foothills of the Sierra
Nevada Mountain range is often slow
going for RVers, but the scenic rewards
are endless.

The End of a Busy Day.
A weary traveler takes time out after a
full day of exploring the shops and
sights of Columbia State Historic Park.

there was considerable gun play that left a haze of smoke lingering over the scene.

As the Main Street show broke up I headed across the highway to get a closer look at old Whistling Billy, a restored steam locomotive that was used to haul ore from the nearby Mary Harrison Mine over a four-mile stretch of track called the "crookedest railroad in the world." From the old locomotive that marks Coulterville's town square, it is just a few steps to the newly opened museum housed in the old stone building that was once the Wells Fargo office. Now officially called the Northern Mariposa County History Center, the museum houses an excellent collection of artifacts of Coulterville's early days, as well as various memorabilia of county history.

Old Church.
This little red church in Sonora is just one of the bustling town's many old buildings attractive to tourists who want to step back in time.

At the museum I had the good fortune to meet Ross Miller, then president of the county historical society, who handed me a card that proclaimed him "Mayor of Jackass Ridge." One of the true characters of contemporary Coulterville, Ross, who would have been right at home here in 1849, explained later that Jackass Ridge was the name given to the knoll where he and his wife built their home before retiring here a number of years before.

After guiding me through some of the exhibits, Ross suggested we take a ride along some of the local backroads. Outside we got into Ross's shiny Lincoln and began a hair-raising ride through the surrounding countryside, over roads that I'm not sure I would have had the courage to take a Jeep. As I clung to the seat and cinched my seat belt tighter, Ross showed me ruins of old mines, brush-covered hills that were sites of historic events, and gave me a running narrative of early Mariposa County life. Back at the museum parking lot, with my feet once again on firm ground, Ross pointed out the old "hangin' tree" that shades Whistling Billy. Our tour continued up Main Street, past the stately, old Jeffrey Hotel, built as a cantina in the 1840s and converted to a hotel in 1852, and several other old buildings that have been restored and now house restaurants and shops. Before returning to his duties at the museum, Ross invited me into the quaint Magnolia Saloon where we paused for a cup of coffee and he filled me in on the ambitious plans the historical society has for further restoration of Coulterville. By now I assume many of those plans have been put into action, making this an even more attractive stopover for enthusiasts of Mother Lode history.

Sonora

Leaving Coulterville reluctantly, I once again pointed my motorhome north along the route of the forty-niners, passing through Chinese Camp and Jamestown as I wound through the Sierra foothills to Sonora. At Chinese Camp I paused long enough to look at the historic post office that sadly has now been abandoned in favor of a more modern facility nearby. At Jamestown, a thriving community of more than 2,000, I paused long enough to have lunch at the historic Hotel Willow and browse through a few of the antique shops.

Five minutes north of Jamestown I entered the outskirts of Sonora. With a population of nearly 4,000, Sonora is the southern Mother Lode's largest community and the the seat of Tuolumne County government. Because of its narrow streets, driving through this bustling community can be a real nightmare for RVers, and you can expect traffic at times to approach that of rush hour on the worst of Southern California's freeways. For those who want to spend some time exploring Sonora's picturesque business district I suggest you find a parking spot (not always easy) on one of the side streets and then walk back to the main thoroughfare, Washington Street.

Worth taking the time to explore in Sonora is the Tuolumne County Museum, housed in an old building originally constructed in 1857.

Charles Moore

Hill Town.
Named for the Mexican state from which many of its early settlers came, Sonora is now one of the most thriving and liveliest communities in the southern Mother Lode. It actually sits on seven small wooded hills and is the seat of Tuolumne County.

Among the museum exhibits are the usual gold-rush memorabilia, an excellent collection of old firearms, and a reconstructed jail cell block. Since the museum is also home to the local chamber of commerce, this is a good spot to pick up brochures and other information on the area. Also of interest here are the Old Gunn House, Sonora's oldest residence (1850) located on Washington Street at the south end of town; the I.O.O.F. Hall (1853) at the north end of Washington; and St. Patrick's Catholic Church (1862), one block west of the courthouse on Jackson Street.

Columbia

After a short stop in Sonora, I headed north to the turnoff leading to Columbia, the historically significant gold-rush town that has been painstakingly restored and is now maintained as a state historic park. In its prime Columbia yielded nearly $90 million in gold, earning the title of "Gem of the Southern Mines," and gained prominence as the most important of the towns that sprang up in the southern Mother Lode.

Architectural Gem or Mistake?
A restored Sonoran Victorian home epit-omizes the grand style of architecture once popular in the area. Although lovingly preserved today, this style has been called "The Tubercular Style" by one critic and a "mistake" by another.

Tuolomne County Visitors' Bureau

Assay Office.
After striking pay dirt, a stop at the assayer's office was a must before mov-ing on to a celebration at the local saloon.

Columbia's origins date to March of 1850 when Dr. Thaddeus Hildreth and his brother set up camp near the present site of the town and began prospecting the many gulches and ravines in the area. Within days they struck it rich and word of their good fortune quickly spread, bringing hundreds of miners flocking in to share the wealth. A tent town given the temporary name of Hildreth's Diggings quickly sprang up, and, before the year was out, a population of several thousand had prompted the founding of a full-fledged town named Columbia.

By the end of 1852, Columbia was a bustling community of more than 150 stores, shops, and saloons. For more than a decade the town thrived; elegant carriages clattered over cobblestone streets, the local theater offered elaborately staged productions, and four banks were estab-lished, making Columbia an important financial center for the southern mines. Unfortunately, what Columbia didn't have was a location near a ready source of water.

In the ensuing years, as the gold gradually played out, Columbia was battered by drought and fire. Despite the establishment in 1854 of a water company that built a system to serve the town and help fight fires, and despite the replacement of burned structures with brick buildings and fireproof iron doors, Columbia, like most of the other towns of the Mother Lode, began a slow decline. By the 1860s most of the miners had moved on, and by the 1870s the town had dropped from a peak popula-tion of nearly 15,000 to a little more than 500.

Today the town has a population of about 350, most of whom make their living serving travelers who come here throughout the year to stroll

A Step Back in Time.
Preserved with remarkable authenticity, the town of Columbia allows visitors to view the gold rush community much as it was during its heyday in the 1850s.

The Old Hoosegow.
Iron doors and bars sturdily anchored in brick and mortar assured that transgressors served their full sentence.

its streets and view the well-preserved remnants of days gone by. Walking along deeply shaded Main Street, which is closed to all motorized traffic, provides you with an unparalleled opportunity to see what it was like to live in a gold rush community of the 1850s. In fact, the atmosphere is so rich with history you can almost hear the ghosts of the past.

Among the ghosts that one is likely to encounter here is that of John Barclay, a victim of a lynch mob in 1852. As the story goes, Barclay, a saloonkeeper, was defending the honor of his wife, Martha, who had been insulted by a a very inebriated fellow named John Huron Smith. Smith had stopped by the Barclay's saloon and entered into an argument with Martha; he made the mistake of slapping her just as Barclay came through the saloon door. Seeing what had transpired, Barclay pulled his gun and killed Smith on the spot.

Ordinarily the code of the frontier would have judged such a killing justified. Unfortunately for Barclay, however, Smith had friends in high places in the fledgling state government. Also, neither of the Barclays was particularly well liked. Once word of Smith's death reached Sacramento, State Senator J. W. Coffroth rode to Columbia, addressed a gathering

Fallon Hotel and Theater.
Hungry for entertainment, miners came to the Fallon Theater from the surrounding gold fields to enjoy performances by traveling theatrical troupes. Performances are still scheduled regularly.

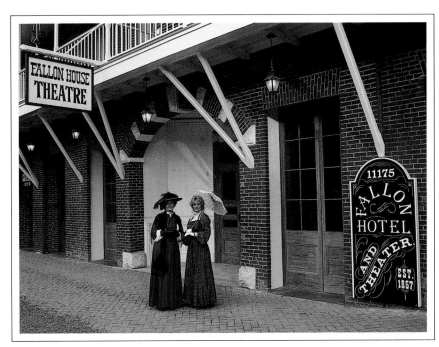

Charles Moore

mob, and demanded immediate justice. Inflamed by Coffroth's impassioned words, the mob descended on the jail where Barclay was being held, removed him from his cell, and carried him down to the end of Gold Springs Road. There they threw a rope over the end of a towering gold flume and strung him up.

Today, the closest Columbia comes to violence are the mock stagecoach robberies presented during the summer for tourists who ride the stage on its loop tour around the park. For those seeking less raucous entertainments a leisurely stroll down Main Street will take you past the Wells Fargo office, the stagecoach depot, the courthouse, the City Hotel, the blacksmith shop, and the fire station. Park headquarters is located in a museum on the corner of Main and State streets.

Because of Columbia's many attractions I would suggest you allow at least a full day to explore the town. Besides the old buildings, most of which now house tourist-oriented businesses such as souvenir shops and candy and antique stores, the town also boasts several restaurants ranging from sandwich shops to the elegant dining room of the City Hotel. I stopped for a brief lunch at the Columbia House Restaurant and found the menu selection and food to be very good. Formal entertainment is offered during the summer months in stage productions at the Fallon House Theater and at the High Society Saloon in the basement of the Magendie Building. Demonstrations of gold panning and blacksmithing skills are also conducted throughout the summer months. A rowdy Fireman's Muster is held in the park every year in May, an event that features a number of brightly colored antique fire wagons along with demonstrations and competitions among firemen who come from all over California for the weekend gathering. It should be noted that the park is open year-round on a daily basis. As might be expected it can be crowded in the summer and RV parking can be a bit scarce during the height of the tourist season. I have visited here several times and found the spring and fall months to be ideal for avoiding crowds and assuring adequate parking for my rig. There are two very good private RV camp-grounds located close to the park. No matter what time of year, if you are planning a weekend visit I would suggest a call ahead for reservations.

Angels Camp

Returning to SR 49 from Columbia, the highway resumes its up-and-down, winding progress through the foothills as it snakes the sixteen miles to Angels Camp. Along this route you'll pass by the village of Tuttletown, a wide spot in the road that contains a few ruins from gold-rush days. One mile past Tuttletown there is a paved side road that cuts three-quarters of a mile east to the site of Mark Twain's cabin on Jackass Hill. During his stay here in 1864 and 1865, Twain reportedly wrote *The Celebrated Jumping Frog of Calaveras County* and *Roughing It*.

Angels Camp Museum.
For anyone who visits California's Southern Mother Lode, a visit to the Angels Camp Museum is a must, if for nothing more than to view the wide variety of mining artifacts and other reminders of the gold rush.

Back on SR 49, after few miles, the highway crosses a bridge high above the Stanislaus River Gorge, then rises into pastureland before reaching the hamlet of Carson Hill. A stop here will give you an opportunity to visit the site of the Morgan Mine, which yielded a spectacular 195-pound nugget in 1854.

From Carson Hill it's just a few minutes before you reach the southern city limits of Angels Camp, the setting for Twain's famous story about the celebrated jumping frog, and the current home of the Annual Jumping Frog Jubilee in May. Long before Twain immortalized this small mountain community, however, Angels Camp was just one more Mother Lode town founded on the promise of sudden riches from a nearby gold strike. Named for George Angel, a merchant who established a trading post here in 1849, Angels Camp rose to early prominence in the wake of a gold discovery that eventually brought some 5,000 miners into the town. Just as the gold from that initial strike began to play out, another major find was made by a fellow with the unlikely name of Bennager Rasberry, and the town continued to thrive through the 1850s.

Now Angels Camp has a population of nearly 3,000 and is one of the busiest communities in the Mother Lode. Although a lot of the buildings along the main thoroughfare have been remodeled over the years to accommodate contemporary businesses, some of the gold-rush quaint-ness remains. Be prepared to be overwhelmed by frogs, though. There are frog signs, and green frogs painted on the sidewalks, and even a bronze statue of a frog in the town square. An interesting stop here is the Angels Camp Museum at the junction of SR 49 and SR 4. Inside the museum numerous artifacts recall Angels Camp's halcyon days, and one will find the expected memorabilia of Mark Twain and another famous writer who spent a good deal of time here, Bret Harte. On the grounds there are some excellent displays of restored mining equipment.

These mighty trees belong to the silences and the milleniums. They seem indeed to be forms of immortality, standing here among the transitory shapes of time.

Edwin Markham (1852-1940)

Unless you're fond of crowds or have a frog to enter in the jumping frog contest, I would suggest you try to avoid Angels Camp during the competition held during the third weekend in May. The rest of the year, the town can be explored at a leisurely pace, and RVers should not have any problem finding adequate parking. I especially recommend a spring-time visit in late April when the surrounding hillsides are a lush green and dotted with wildflowers.

"Biggest Trees I Ever See'd"

While Angels Camp generally marks the terminus of a tour known as The Southern Mines, no visit here would be complete without a side trip out of town to Calaveras Big Trees State Park. Reached by driving east on SR 4 and following its winding course as it climbs toward the peaks of the Sierra Nevada Mountain Range, this magnificent park is only about thirty miles from SR 49 and well worth the forty-five-minute drive. Along the way take some time to explore some of the old structures in the quaint mountain community of Murphys.

Often called the most impressive of the Sierra redwoods, the giant trees of the Calaveras park were discovered in 1852 by a professional hunter, A. T. Dowd, who came upon the trees while pursuing a wounded grizzly. He rushed back to Murphys with the story of a grove of trees "taller than the masts of ships and thicker than houses," and was promptly dismissed as just another addlepated wanderer with a tall tale. Undaunted, Dowd finally managed to trick some of the townsfolk into climbing the mountains with him by telling them he had located the grizzly — "The biggest I ever see'd" — and needed some help bringing it into town. Once others had seen the trees and confirmed Dowd's story, word of the forest of giant trees quickly spread, drawing numerous travelers who made the arduous trek up the mountain.

Put under state protection in 1954, the sequoias of Calaveras Big Trees State Park are now divided into North and South Groves that total 5,994 acres. During the summer months park rangers conduct campfire programs and lead highly informative interpretive hikes through the forests. A number of trails wind through both sections of the park, the self-guiding nature walk in the North Grove being the most popular. The biggest tree here is the Empire State, measuring nineteen feet in diameter. The South Grove, reached via a winding paved road that leads out of park headquarters, boasts the largest tree in the park, the Louis Agassiz, measuring twenty-two feet in diameter.

The park is open year-round and offers two campgrounds — North Grove and Squaw Hollow — as well as several picnic areas. No hookups are available. In the winter heavy snowfalls may close the road into the park intermittently so it's best to call for current conditions if you plan a visit at that time of year. Also, since the elevation here ranges from 3,500 to 5,500 feet, make sure you have plenty of propane for your rig's furnace, warm blankets for your bed, and suitable clothes and boots for trekking through the snow.

POINTS OF INTEREST: California Tour 6

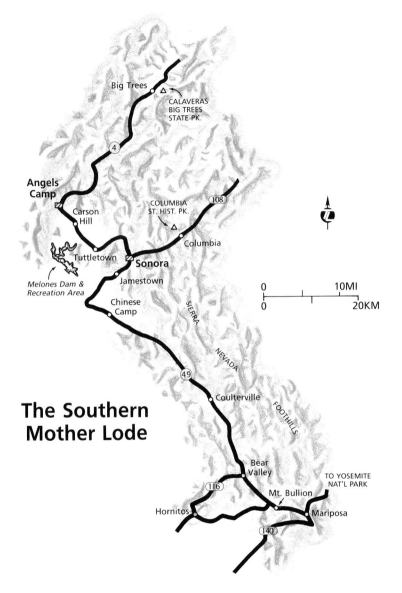

The Southern Mother Lode

Coulterville: *Country Fair and Antique Show,* May; *Gold Rush Days Celebration,* May; *Fireman's Barbecue,* July; *Bluegrass and Country Western Jamboree,* August.

Mariposa: *Mariposa County Fair,* September.

Sonora: *Mother Lode Fair,* July.

MUSEUMS:
Angels Camp: *Angels Camp Museum,* SR 49 and SR 4, daily, year-round except for major holidays, (209) 736-2963.

Mariposa: *Mariposa County History Center,* SR 140 at 12th and Jessie streets, daily April–October, weekends only remainder of year; closed January. (209) 966-2924.

Sonora: *Tuolumne County Museum,* 158 W. Bradford Avenue, daily May to September, Monday–Friday remainder of year, (209) 532-1317.

SPECIAL ATTRACTIONS:
Angels Camp: *Outdoor Adventure River Specialists (OARS),* Box 67, Angels Camp, California 95222, (209) 736-4677.

OUTFITTERS:
Angels Camp: Outdoor Adventure River Specialists (OARS), Box 67, Angels Camp, California 95222, (209) 736-4677.

RESTAURANTS:
Columbia: *City Hotel,* Main Street, (209) 532-1479, Continental cuisine; *The Columbia House,* corner of State and Main streets, (209) 532-5134, American fare served family style.

Coulterville: *Jeffrey Hotel Restaurant,* 1 Main Street, (209) 878-3471, American.

Mariposa: *Bon Ton Café,* 7301 SR 49 North, (209) 377-8229, American and Guatalmalan cuisine.

ACCESS: North on *SR 99* to *SR 140* at Merced; east on *SR 140* to Mariposa, then north on *SR 49.*

INFORMATION: *Mariposa County Chamber of Commerce,* 5158 Hwy 140, Mariposa, California 95338, (209) 966-2456; *Tuolomne County Chamber of Commerce,* P.O. Box 277, Sonora, California 95370, (209) 532-4212; *Calaveras County Cham-* *ber of Commerce,* P.O. Box 177, San Andreas, California 95249, (209) 754-1821.

ANNUAL EVENTS:
Angels Camp: *Calaveras County Fair and Jumping Frog Jubilee,* May; *Mountain Aire Rock Festival,* May; *July Fourth Celebration,* July; *Fireman's Fun Day,* August; *Frog Town Peddler's Fair,* September; *Pumpkin Day,* October.

The Central Coast

Santa Barbara . . . lies basking in the southern sun with the blue waters of the bay rippling at her feet and her head pillowed on the foothills of the Santa Ynez Mountains . . . there are no seasons. . . . Two miles back from the sea . . . is the mission [standing] as a watch and ward over all Santa Barbara — a thing of beauty to the eye and a reminder of a day and a dynasty gone by.

Benjamin Cummings Truman (1835-1916)
pioneer journalist in the Los Angeles *Star*

Ask any Northern Californian and he'll tell you Santa Barbara represents the last bastion of sophistication before the traveler descends into the (alleged) cultural wasteland of Southern California. While that view is a bit harsh, there's no denying that this quaint seaside city — and much of the surrounding area — have a distinct charm not found in the casual atmosphere of the sun-drenched locales farther south.

Last Remnant of the Lost Paradise

Santa Barbara has long enjoyed a reputation as one of Southern California's most congenial vacation spots. Even the Spanish explorers, who established a presidio here in 1782, recognized the region's special allure, dubbing it *la tierra adorado* (the beloved land).

Situated between the Pacific coast and the scenic Santa Ynez mountain range, the city of 75,000 grew from its military outpost origins to a mission settlement under the guidance of Father Fermin Francisco de Lasuen. By the beginning of this century, its near-perfect climate (daytime highs in the mid-70s and lows in the mid-60s) had earned Santa Barbara its reputation as an idyllic retreat. The wealthy of Los Angeles made it their weekend watering hole and well-to-do retirees flocked to its milder climate. Santa Barbara thus became a sedate, sophisticated hideaway, renowned for its palm-lined beaches and quaint Spanish colonial architecture of red-tiled roofs, white stucco walls, rounded archways, and iron grillwork.

Santa Barbara today has been called the last remnant of the lost paradise of California. Most residents strongly agree and jealously guard the city's growth, architecture, and heritage — which is a big plus for travelers who come here to explore the reminders of the early Spanish settlers, enjoy the varied cultural offerings, or simply relax on Santa Barbara's sparkling clean beaches.

A stop at the Santa Barbara Convention and Visitors Bureau (1330 State Street) in the heart of the city's historic El Paseo (downtown) district is probably the best way to start a tour here. A word of warning, however: Though this area was completely revamped about eighteen years ago to better accommodate tourists, not much thought was given to the fact that some visitors might be driving RVs. As a result, parking for large motorhomes is scarce, but lots can be found on the fringes of the downtown district that will hold a large motorhome and still allow an easy walk to State Street.

At the bureau, pick up a walking tour map of the Paseo, as well as the Red-Tile-Tour map that will direct you on a twenty four-mile scenic loop around the city. Up along State you'll find a number of interesting craft shops, some excellent art galleries (I particularly liked the Keystone

Tour 7 *84 miles*
Side trip to Los Padres National Forest Camp, 25 miles

SANTA BARBARA • SANTA BARBARA MISSION • COLD SPRINGS CANYON • LAKE CACHUMA • SANTA YNEZ VALLEY • LOS PADRES NATIONAL FOREST • LOS OLIVOS • BALLARD • MISSION SANTA INES • SOLVANG • BUELLTON • LOMPOC • LA PURÍSIMA CONCEPCIÓN MISSION

Harbor Scenes.
Cool ocean breezes and views of sailboats gliding on the calm waters of Santa Barbara Harbor are just some of the pleasures awaiting visitors to California's central coast.

County Courthouse.
The beautifully landscaped grounds of the Santa Barbara County Courthouse include graceful palms, lush sunken gardens, and a lovely fountain.

Gallery tucked back off a little covered walkway), and some very fine restaurants. On the corner, where State meets Anapamu Street, there is the small Museum of Art building, which houses an impressive variety of traveling exhibits along with permanent collections of Oriental and American art. The main gallery showcases Egyptian, Greek, and Roman sculptures, which on clear days are dramatically lighted by shafts of light streaming down from the skylights. Just a block away from the museum is the Santa Barbara County Courthouse (Anapamu and Santa Barbara streets), a huge building of Spanish-Moorish design built in 1929. Besides being the largest building in the city, this imposing structure houses a number of beautiful murals that colorfully depict the history of Santa Barbara and the surrounding area.

The Mission

The story outlined in the murals is a good introduction to the city's historical centerpiece, the magnificent Santa Barbara Mission (featured on the cover), which can be reached by driving northwest on Santa

Mediterranean Architecture.
Visitors who ride the clock-tower elevator to the top of the County Courthouse enjoy a panoramic view of Santa Barbara's many red tile roofs and the surrounding area.

Barbara Street to Mission Street, turning right, and following Mission to Laguna Street. The mission, built in 1820 after earthquakes destroyed three earlier buildings, is commonly called the "Queen of the Missions" because its matching bell towers and Roman-temple facade have made it a standout in the twenty-one-mission chain.

In addition to admiring the beauty of the exterior and interior structures, I found the guided tour of the mission grounds absolutely fascinating. An explanation of the mission's elaborate water system, which consists of an intricate network of dams, reservoirs, and aqueducts, will leave you with a deep appreciation of the ingenuity of the mission leaders and the skill of the Canalino Indians who actually accomplished much of the labor. Incidentally, it's also interesting to learn that the mission fathers had a rather special view of their responsibilities to their Indian charges. Although the missions were ostensibly established to pacify the Indians and provide them with the skills to settle the land and guide their own destinies, the padres often guided this transition with an iron hand. For instance, once an Indian came to live on the mission grounds and was baptized, he could never again return to his former life. Those who tried were hunted down by the Spanish soldiers and forcibly returned to the mission compound.

Mission Santa Barbara.
The "Queen of the Missions" was established in 1786 by the Franciscan Fathers, tenth in the chain of twenty-one California missions.

The Museum of Natural History

From the mission it's only a short drive to the Museum of Natural History (on Puesta del Sol Road), which is worth a stop to view the excellent exhibits on Canalino Indian culture dating back before the arrival of the Spanish settlers. A few miles farther north on Mission Canyon Road you'll find the Santa Barbara Botanic Garden, a seventy-five-acre facility featuring displays of indigenous California vegetation, ranging from giant redwoods to cactus and wildflowers. For those who want to linger, there is a beautiful and informative walk along the five-mile trail that winds through the gardens and past an old dam and aqueduct that once served the mission.

The Streets of Santa Barbara

It should be noted that driving an RV to and from the mission along some of the side streets, and particularly the winding Mission Canyon Road, requires some caution because of the narrow streets and cross traffic. You'll want to take things slow, though, because the area up around the mission and gardens is one of the most scenic in Santa Barbara. In fact, if you want to make an exceptionally scenic side trip when coming back from the gardens, turn east on Foothill Road (SR 192) and wind along the tree-shaded road through a section that contains some of Santa Barbara's most magnificent and stately old homes.

If you choose to take this drive, you can continue along Foothill until it becomes Sycamore Canyon Road and curves south to intersect US 101. From there, turn west and exit at Cabrillo Boulevard to start your drive along the Santa Barbara beachfront. Again, like the downtown area,

Natural History Museum.
The huge skeleton of a blue whale dwarfs visitors to Santa Barbara's Museum of Natural History.

95

Scenic Residential Area.
Many of Santa Barbara's best preserved and most beautiful old homes are found near the mission.

Michele Burgess

parking here is at a premium for RVs (the weekends in the summer months can be nearly impossible). I found the paid parking lots along Cabrillo, just before the intersection with Santa Barbara Street, are a good compromise because they allow access to Chase Palm Park and are within easy walking distance of Stearns Wharf. Those whose vehicles permit can also find paid parking on the wharf itself, but trailers and large motorhomes are not allowed.

Legend of the Dolphins

Along the park's narrow strip of grass are a few fire pits and tables for beachside picnics and a wide strip of sand for sunning. At the entrance to the wharf stands a two-tiered fountain with three dolphins leaping from the bubbling water in the middle of the upper tier. At the time of my visit, the fountain was a little more than a year old and the controversy surrounding its construction was gradually fading at the same time the legend of the miracle of the dolphins was growing.

Dolphin Fountain.
The graceful dolphin fountain is situated at the foot of Stearns Wharf. Controversy surrounded the construction of the fountain, but it has become an accepted part of the Santa Barbara scene.

Michele Burgess

The idea for a fountain was born in 1980 following the resurrection of the wharf after it was destroyed by a fire in the late 1970s. The fountain was suggested as a symbol of welcome to tourists and was originally designed in the shape of a champagne glass in the midst of which, according to the original proposal, "would be a young, thinly clad woman holding a palm frond." The inscription on the fountain would read: "May All Your Days Be Filled with Loving Moments, Gentle Smiles, and the Joy of Friendship."

Despite the good intentions of the original planners, the idea of the "friendship fountain" and the "thinly clad woman" didn't catch on with Santa Barbara residents. The proposed design brought only a smattering of contributions, so city officials scrapped that plan and came up with the

Michele Burgess

Stearns Wharf.
The Sea Center on Stearns Wharf features an aquarium and a museum depicting various aspects of the marine world.

idea for a bicentennial fountain to commemorate Santa Barbara's founding. A design competition was held and *Dolphins,* submitted by local sculptor Bud Bottoms, was the hands-down winner. Despite that overwhelming victory, however, actual construction of the fountain became mired in local politics and petty bickering about the appropriateness of the design. Consequently, the dedication didn't take place until 1985, three full years after the city's official bicentennial celebration.

And therein lie the roots of the fountain's growing legend. During the squabbling over the design, someone discovered the Rainbow Bridge fable, an old Chumash Indian legend of Hutash, the earth goddess. The story goes that Hutash, in an effort to relieve the overpopulation of the nearby Santa Cruz Islands, prepared to lead some of her subjects to the mainland via the Rainbow Bridge. Those making the journey were commanded not to look down, but of course some disobeyed and promptly fell into the sea. Though they were forever lost to the tribe, Hutash took pity on them and turned them into dolphins.

In keeping with the legend and Santa Barbara's Chumash heritage, the dedication ceremony for the fountain included an Indian priest who blew incense from a conch shell and invoked the blessing of "Father Sun and Mother Moon." At the moment the priest was calling on his Chumash ancestors, a number of local residents swear, some 100 yards offshore, a large school of bottlenose dolphins appeared and popped their smiling beaks out of the water. A new legend, that of the miracle of the dolphins, was born.

Did the dolphins actually appear offshore? I asked that question of a number of people sitting around the fountain and got an answer from a distinguished-looking, gray-haired gentleman who told me he came to the wharf nearly every day. "You bet," he said. "It was the darndest thing.

Moreton Bay Fig.
The *Guinness Book of World Records* estimates that this huge specimen, brought to Santa Barbara from Australia as a seedling in 1876, can shade 10,000 people at high noon.

Michele Burgess

Michele Burgess

Yacht Harbor.
Hundreds of sailboats and yachts, as well as Santa Barbara's colorful fishing fleet, are sheltered behind the breakwater.

The day before the dedication the weather was overcast and things looked pretty gloomy. But the day the fountain was blessed the sky was bright blue, and it looked like you could reach out and touch the islands. And you could see the dolphins just as clearly — swarms of them. There must have been a hundred or more."

Regardless of the truth of the story, the fountain is an interesting attraction and certainly a handsome introduction to the wharf itself. A stroll out to the end of the pier takes you to a variety of shops and gives a commanding view of the harbor. For me, a highlight here is the Harbor Restaurant, another Santa Barbara landmark that was a victim of the wharf fire, but one that, happily, was reestablished when the wharf was reopened. As might be expected, the Harbor's seafood dishes are excellent, with the lobster and bouillabaisse rating rave reviews.

Continuing west on Cabrillo Boulevard, you follow the coastline past the Naval Reserve Training Center, the Santa Barbara Yacht Club, and Shoreline Park until the street changes to Shoreline Drive, then Cliff Drive, and Las Palmas Drive as it swings north to link up with US 101. A little more than a mile farther west on 101, take the SR 154 off-ramp that cuts north to scenic San Marcos Pass.

A Tavern in the Canyon

For the first few miles the San Marcos Pass road is a wide four-lane highway as it winds toward the Santa Ynez foothills. But it quickly changes to a narrow, steep two-lane highway as it climbs toward the summit (2,224 feet). The grade makes it slow going for large motorhomes and those pulling big trailers, but thankfully the climb to the summit is a short one. One can only imagine what the climb was like for those in an earlier era when this was the main north-south stagecoach route.

Just past the summit you'll find a quaint reminder of the earlier days if you take a little side trip that loops through Cold Spring Canyon under the massive Cold Spring Arch Bridge, the largest arched span in the western United States. Nestled within this narrow, tree-shaded canyon is a complex of old buildings that made up the stagecoach stop more than 100 years ago. The log structures, which consist of a hall now used for an occasional theater performance, a tavern, an antique shop, and an old jail, are now owned by Audrey Ovington, a good-natured and colorful Santa Barbara antique collector, who has done her best to keep everything as authentic as possible.

Surprisingly, this historic spot remains one of the region's best-kept secrets. You won't find it listed in most tour guides or noted on most maps. No doubt because of the good food at the Cold Spring Tavern, however, it's a popular stopover for locals. That makes parking a problem for RVs, but if you arrive after the noon crush you may find some room in the parking lot. If not, a couple of wide spots in the road around the bend from the tavern will accommodate some rigs and still allow an easy walk back to the tavern.

From the stagecoach stop, just about a half mile past the Cold Spring Bridge, Paradise Road cuts off to the right and follows a narrow, winding

Cold Spring Arch Bridge.
A graceful green arch, the largest in the western United States, spans rugged Cold Spring Canyon.

Cold Spring Tavern.
When the San Marcos Pass toll road was completed in the 1880s, a small restaurant was built in Cold Spring Canyon to serve stagecoach passengers.

Lake Cachuma County Park.
The campground at Lake Cachuma features spacious, shaded sites with picnic and barbecue facilities.

route to dead-end on the banks of the Santa Ynez River. The best time for a visit here is the spring or late fall when the fire danger is low and the road is open all the way to the river. A couple of scenic, oak-shaded county campgrounds, with sites that can accommodate rigs of moderate size, are tucked back here, but none are on the river, so if you plan to fish you'll have to drive. The extra effort may be worth it since the ranger at the nearby Los Prietos Ranger Station told me the river is stocked regularly with good-sized trout.

Lake Cachuma

Although the drive up Paradise Road is a pleasant detour, about eleven miles up the road the campsites at Lake Cachuma are more spacious and the lake offers some excellent fishing for rainbow and Kamloops trout. Tackle and boat rentals are available, and there is also a snack bar and a store that stocks groceries and tackle. A word of warning: The store prices are a bit steep, so I would advise stocking up on the essentials before you leave Santa Barbara. Also, the lake is open to fishing only; waterskiing and swimming are not allowed since the lake supplies drinking water for Santa Barbara.

During the summer months especially, advance reservations for both boats and campsites at Cachuma are advised as the facility draws heavy crowds of Los Angeles weekenders. Full hookups are available in some overnight sites set aside in a year-round residential area just inside the park entrance. Even without hookups, I found the sites on the upper peninsula more desirable because they are away from the noise of the main campground. Here you can park under the spreading limbs of a

Lake Cachuma.
This man-made lake, which takes its name from a Chumash Indian village that once stood here, offers good fishing and boating.

Michele Burgess

Michele Burgess

Horse Country.
Several sprawling ranches in the fertile Santa Ynez Valley breed magnificent thoroughbred racehorses.

California oak and enjoy the full effect of the beautiful sunsets that fall across the lake.

As SR 154 continues past Cachuma, it dips and rises and then drops into the open ranchland of the Santa Ynez Valley. Ever since its discovery by Spanish explorers in 1769, the valley has been cattle-and-horse country. The tradition remains today, with several of the ranches owned by families who trace their history in the valley back to the early 1800s.

The mineral content of the valley soil is said to produce a grass that is especially good for building strong bones in thoroughbred horses. Thus many of the ranches are major breeding operations for some of the nation's finest racehorses. A side trip up Armour Ranch Road, about four miles past the Cachuma entrance, leads through some of the valley's most prosperous ranch operations.

The Wilderness of Los Padres

For a real contrast, turn off Armour Ranch Road to Happy Canyon Road and follow it along an oak-shaded lane that winds past whitewashed fences and green pasturelands to climb into the mountains of the San

Ballard School.
Framed by a pair of black walnut trees, this little red two-room schoolhouse has been in continuous use since 1883.

Mission Santa Ines.
This old mission, founded in 1804 just outside where Solvang now lies, owned 12,000 head of stock at the peak of its prosperity.

Rafael and Sierra Madre ranges. Once it begins its climb into the mountains, the route is slow going, with a couple of tight switchbacks that require careful maneuvering (drivers of big rigs may want to think twice), but within a few miles the rolling grasslands give way to oak- and pine-covered slopes. In a little more than half an hour, you're deep in the Los Padres National Forest on the edge of the San Rafael and Santa Lucia Wilderness areas. Several U.S. Forest Service campgrounds are here, most of which have spaces to accommodate fairly large RVs. During times of high fire danger in midsummer and early fall, the entire region may be closed to traffic, so check at Cachuma first or call the Los Padres headquarters in Santa Barbara before making the trip.

In both spring and late fall, when the fire danger is low and the countryside is at its greenest, this side trip offers a quiet respite from the bustling civilization that lies only a few miles away. Its designation as a wilderness region is well earned. As I drove the dirt road past the Figueroa Ranger Station to Ballard Campground, I was forced to stop to let a small herd of deer amble across the road. Just about 100 yards farther on, I paused to watch a bobcat slip quietly through the trees along the edge of the road.

The return trip to the valley can be made by either backtracking or continuing along Figueroa Mountain Road, which loops back through the town of Los Olivos and links up with the main highway. If you decide to take this route, I recommend a stop in Los Olivos at the historic Mattei's Tavern, which was built in 1886 as a stop for the Butterfield Stage Lines. This small town of only 800 population has recently become a popular retreat for artists, and a number of local galleries display their work. The region immediately surrounding Los Olivos is also emerging as a wine-producing area. A resident told me nearly twenty wineries are now operating around the town, many of which offer tours.

From Los Olivos you can take Grand Avenue/Pintado Road through Ballard — the oldest community in the valley — directly into Solvang. A short stop in Ballard will give you time to see the little red Ballard School, built in 1883 and wonderfully preserved as a school that now serves kindergarten through third grade.

Hidden Gem of the Missions

Before heading into Solvang, I stopped on the outskirts to see Mission Santa Ines. This mission, the nineteenth, founded in 1804, is one of the few named in honor of a woman, Saint Agnes, a Roman martyr who died in A.D. 304. Despite the fact that it was off the beaten path, Mission Santa Ines was one of the most prosperous in the mission chain and housed a large Indian population that tended 13,000 head of cattle, cultivated fields of crops, and produced crafts that became renowned throughout the region. This mission also has the unique distinction of being the site of a major Indian revolt in 1824, in which a number of Indians died fighting the oppression of their Spanish masters.

Though peace was restored quickly, the mission's prosperity began to decline, and many of the buildings fell into disrepair when the Spanish governor, Pio Pico, ordered the dismantling of the missions. Restoration began as early as 1904, but serious work to return the mission to its original state was undertaken only in 1947. Now this "hidden gem of the missions" has a spotless facade that features a long, arch-lined walkway, a pointed tile roof, and a campanile with three bells that rises above a small Indian graveyard. Inside the church are some outstanding murals, and other buildings house a museum and a variety of Indian artifacts.

A Bit of Denmark

The mission's tree- and fence-lined lane leads back to SR 246, the main east-west thoroughfare that runs through the quaint community of Solvang, which translates from the Danish as "sunny valley." For my tastes, Solvang may be a bit too quaint, looking somewhat like a Hollywood set designer's idea of a Scandinavian town. Still there is an unmistakable charm to Solvang's old-world cobblestone walks, windmills, cross-beamed walls, and thatchlike roofs with wooden storks mounted on their peaks. Danish bakeries are everywhere and the aroma of fresh pastry spills into the streets, tempting visitors to come inside. You can also browse in a number of crafts and curio shops that emphasize items such as cuckoo clocks and Danish apparel. Each year in September the town harkens back to its heritage with a Danish Days festival that features costumed dancers and musicians who wander the streets entertaining visitors.

About three miles west of Solvang, across US 101, lies the tiny town of Buellton, home of the famous Pea Soup Andersen's Restaurant. This

Michele Burgess

Danish Days in Solvang.
On the third weekend in September each year, Solvang celebrates its Danish heritage with entertainment, dancing, special foods, and a parade.

A Danish Village.
Solvang, meaning "sunny valley," by 1914 had become a cultural center and gathering place for Danish people on the West Coast.

Michele Burgess

Flowers of All Hue.
The backroads near Lompoc offer the traveler an unparalled vista of flower fields in spring.

landmark restaurant was established by the Andersen family some fifty years ago. I'm sure pea soup connoisseurs will find the soup exceptional, but the restaurant also serves up a variety of very good luncheon and dinner fare at moderate prices. Youngsters will be delighted with the restaurant's well-stocked basement toy shop.

Besides Andersen's there are a few other good restaurants in Buellton, as well as a couple of large private campgrounds. I checked into the Flying Flags Travel Park, a large, well-maintained campground conveniently located near US 101, just off SR 246.

Flower Capital of the World

From Buellton, a fifteen-mile drive west on SR 246 takes you to Lompoc (pronounced lom-poke), a town that boasts the title of Flower Seed Capital of the World and is also the site of La Purísima Concepción Mission. Located on the outskirts of town, this 966-acre facility is operated by the California Department of Parks and Recreation and is said to offer the most complete and accurate depiction of mission life.

Originally founded in 1789 and moved to the present site in 1815, this mission is unique owing to its heavily reinforced buildings to ward off earthquake damage, as well as an overall design that facilitated escape in the event of a catastrophic quake. The ranger here led me on a tour through several buildings, which include displays on hide tanning, a re-created tallow works, a weavery where wool and cotton were processed into blankets and clothing, an olive crusher, and a beautifully manicured garden. All of these displays come alive in May when costumed participants gather for the La Purísima Mission Fiesta.

Michele Burgess

La Purísima Mission.
Built in the early 1800s, La Purísima Concepción represents one of California's most complete and authentic examples of mission life and architecture.

In the town of Lompoc I was directed to the museum, which is operated by the local historical society. In addition to general exhibits depicting development of the area from the mission days to the establishment of nearby Vandenberg Air Force Base, the museum houses an impressive array of Indian artifacts and has a number of superb exhibits on the history of the Chumash and other Indian tribes. Here you can also pick up a map for a nineteen-mile driving tour of the surrounding flower fields.

Lompoc earned its reputation as a major producer of flower seeds when a number of seed companies — Burpee, Bodger, and Denholm, to name a few — located here to take advantage of the region's near-perfect growing conditions. The seeds are planted in the fall, and by May of each year the fields are ablaze with hundreds of acres of sweet pea, larkspur, petunia, aster, marigold, and zinnia blossoms. To celebrate this riot of color, the town holds an annual flower festival on the last full weekend in June. The festival includes a parade with floats decked out in valley-grown blossoms, flower shows, arts-and-crafts booths, a carnival, concerts, and tours of the flower fields in full bloom.

For those who might want to linger a little longer, the city of Lompoc maintains the River Park Campground near the Santa Ynez River. No hookups are available.

Michele Burgess

Poppy Fields.
Springtime in rural Santa Barbara County often finds the hillsides blanketed with wildflowers, especially California poppies.

End of the Loop

Instead of staying over, I elected to head south back toward Santa Barbara, exploring the backcountry along the winding scenic route of SR 1. This road twists and turns for nineteen miles through the rolling foothills of the Santa Ynez Mountains before linking up with US 101 near the Gaviota Pass, just north of Santa Barbara. I didn't try it, but you can take a side trip here on a narrow road that turns southwest and meanders over a small mountain pass (Jualachichi Summit, 1,104 feet) to dead-end at Jalama Beach County Park on the Pacific coast. I asked about the road's condition at the chamber of commerce in town and was told it was passable for RVs. Those wanting to take the trip might want to do a little further checking before proceeding.

In the springtime the green hills, dotted with wild California poppies and bright yellow patches of mustard, were truly a glorious sight as I drove the last few miles back to the main highway. Those who link up with US 101 here have the choice of continuing south to Los Angeles or heading north through the Santa Maria Valley toward San Francisco. No matter which direction you choose, you'll be hard pressed to find the diversity that is contained within this relatively small area. There may be more spectacular ocean vistas to the north and more excitement to the south, but nothing will match the infinite variety of the Central Coast.

POINTS OF INTEREST: California Tour 7

The Central Coast

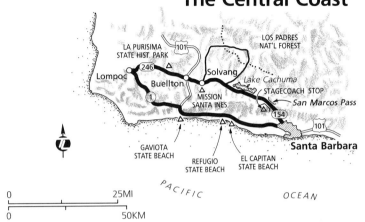

ACCESS: *US 101* at Santa Barbara; *SR 154* north from Santa Barbara to Solvang; *SR 246* to Lompoc; *SR 1* south from Lompoc to *US 101.*

INFORMATION: *Santa Barbara Chamber of Commerce,* 1 South B Street, Santa Barbara, California 93101, (805) 965-3021; *Solvang Chamber of Commerce,* 433 Alisal, Solvang, California 93463, (805) 688-3317; *Lompoc Valley Chamber of Commerce,* 11 South I Street, (805) 736-4567.

ANNUAL EVENTS:
Lompoc: *Vintner's Festival,* May; *Chili Cookoff,* May; *Cinco de Mayo Parade,* May; *Flower Festival,* June; *Arts and Crafts Show,* June; *Mission Life Reenactment,* July–August; *Pioneer Days,* September; *W.C. Fields Festival,* October; *Mission Christmas Program,* December.

Santa Barbara; *Summer Solstice Parade,* June; *National Horse and Flower Show,* July; *Spanish Days Fiesta,* August; *Concours d'Elegance,* September; *Christmas Parade,* December.

Solvang: *Danish Days,* September.

MUSEUMS AND GALLARIES:
Lompoc: *Lompoc Museum,* 200 South H Street, Tuesday–Sunday, year-round, (805) 736-3888.

Santa Barbara: *Museum of Art,* 1130 State Street, Tuesday–Sunday, year-round, closed Easter, Thanksgiving and Christmas, (805) 963-4364; *Santa Barbara Museum of Natural History,* 2559 Puesta del Sol Road, daily, year-round, except major holidays, admission charged, (805) 682-4711; *Historical Society Museum,* 136 East De la Guerra, Tuesday–Sunday, except major holidays, (805) 966-1601.

SPECIAL ATTRACTIONS:
Lompoc: *La Purísima Mission State Historic Park,* four miles NE of town, off SR 246, daily, year-round, except for Easter, Thanksgiving, and Christmas, admission charged for tours, (805) 733-3713.

Santa Barbara: *Mission Santa Barbara,* Los Olivos and Laguna streets, daily, year-round, except for Easter, Thanksgiving, and Christmas, admission charged for tours, (805) 682-4149; *Botanic Garden,* 1212 Mission Canyon Road, daily, year-round, (805) 682-4726.

Solvang: *Old Mission Santa Ines,* 1760 Mission Drive, daily, year-round, except New Year's Day, Easter, Thanksgiving, and Christmas, admission charged, (805) 688-4815.

RESTAURANTS:
Ballard: *Ballard Store Restaurant,* 2449 Baseline Avenue, (805) 688-5319, International cuisine.

Buellton: *Pea Soup Anderson's,* 51 East Highway 246, 1-(800) PEA SOUP.

Santa Barbara: Santa Barbara has a number of fine restaurants, featuring a wide variety of fare at various prices; get a complete listing locally.

Solvang: *Bit 'O Denmark Restaurant,* 473 Alisal Road, (805) 688-5426, Danish and Continental cuisine; *Danish Inn Restaurant,* 1547 Mission Drive, (805) 688-4813, Scandinavian and Continental cuisine; *Møllekroen Restaurant,* 435 Alisal Road, (805) 688-4555, Danish and American menu.

Michele Burgess

The Southern Desert

*These are the gardens of the Desert,
   these
The unshorn fields, boundless and
   beautiful. . . .*

William Cullen Bryant

George Ostertag

Given the population explosion that has beset Southern California in the last twenty-five years, backroading in this region has just about gone the way of the stagecoach and the missionaries. From Los Angeles south, the coast and inland valleys have fallen to real estate developers and industrial growth. With the help of a few urban and suburban parks, the Santa Monica and San Bernardino mountain ranges struggle valiantly to accommodate the weekend onslaught of Southern Californians seeking a brief respite from freeway congestion and the frenzy of city life.

The one exception to all this is the desert expanse that spreads from the eastern foothills of these mountain ranges all the way to the Nevada border. Here, in an area bordered on the north by I-15 and on the south by I-10, lie some 25 million acres of the vast Mojave Desert, offering snowbirds and other winter visitors the opportunity to get away from it all and explore a network of highways, county roads, narrow dirt paths, and rarely traveled trails.

While desert exploration might seem unappealing to many RVers — indeed in the summertime this is a place to avoid — I don't think any visit to the Golden State is complete without taking some time to look beyond the cactus, rocks, and sand and sample a few of the Mojave's riches.

Tour **8** *145 miles*

TWENTYNINE PALMS • JOSHUA TREE NATIONAL MONUMENT • PALM SPRINGS • INDIO

The Mojave Controversy

Because the status of much of the land in this section of the Mojave is now uncertain due to a dispute that has pitted recreation users against conservationists and ecologists, it is difficult to map out a suggested backroad route. That doesn't mean, however, that RVers who take the time to travel to this region are going to find themselves shut out. The pivotal question is how much freedom will RVers and other recreation users of these desert lands have in the future?

At the heart of the dispute is the question of whether this region will continue under the jurisdiction of the Bureau of Land Management (BLM) or the National Park Service (NPS). It's a question that has been debated now for several years and may not be settled for several more. The fact is there is plenty of land to go around, and, no matter what the outcome, this will remain a region of vast recreation potential. If the National Park Service wins in the jurisdictional dispute, RVers will find that camping will be in designated areas only, with access to some backroads eliminated. On the other hand, if the Bureau of Land Management continues as the primary administrator here, RVers will continue to have the freedom to roam at will, explore any road or trail that doesn't have a gate, and stop where they want.

Southern Desert.
Stately and stoic, the ancient Joshua trees have weathered the desert winds and shifting sands through the sunsets of hundreds of years.

Desert Bloom.
Despite the teddy-bear cholla's whimsical name, this desert denizen is far from cuddly. But in spring, triggered by winter rains and sunny days, cacti blossom and become the desert's colorful carpet.

George Ostertag

Flowering Beauty.
Blooming cacti are a reminder that beauty can be found throughout this barren land.

Robert E. Howells

The Charm of the Desert

Even without that debate, the reality is that access and travel in the desert is dynamic, controlled more by the forces of nature than the actions of man. Some graded routes are only temporary, are not maintained, and quickly become impassable. Even maintained gravel and dirt roads often fall victim to desert winds and flash floods. The only thing you can count on is that the paved state and county routes marked on your map are almost always open. Beyond that, expect the unexpected. For me, that challenge is part of the Mojave's considerable charm.

Joshua Tree National Monument

For those who want to take some time to get acclimated to the desert, I recommend you make Joshua Tree National Monument your first stop. Within the monument there are nine campgrounds (no hookups), all of which offer views of the monument's massive rock formations and the spectacular desert sunsets. At the time I was there all the campgrounds were on a first-come-first-served basis. There was some talk, however, of putting in a reservation system, so a phone call in advance might not be a bad idea.

Besides the expected desert flora and fauna, Joshua Tree offers a wide variety of sights and activities within its 467,000 acres. First, be aware that the sprawling monument covers an expanse of the desert that ranges in elevation from 1,000 to 6,000 feet, with many of the roads at the 3,000- to 4,000-foot level. Thus, during the prime snowbird season of roughly October through mid-May, temperatures can be brisk and sometimes downright cold. In the summer, the altitude helps to keep the monu-

Desert Hideaway.
Enclosed by picturesque formations, the campsites in Hidden Valley offer RVers a true desert hideaway.

ment comfortable, but temperatures can still range between the high 80s to 100° plus in the lower elevations. During June, July, and August, temperatures of 115°F — and sometimes higher — are not uncommon on the desert floor. Be prepared.

Start your tour of Joshua Tree by exiting I-10 at the SR 62 turnoff, then travel north through the villages of Morongo Valley, Yucca Valley, Joshua Tree, and Twentynine Palms to the north entrance to the monument. Before entering, however, I suggest a stop at the monument's official visitor center in Twentynine Palms. Here you'll find exhibits on the desert terrain, as well as displays of artifacts. Pick up a few of the free maps and brochures and take the time to browse through the other printed material that is for sale. Much of that offers more detailed information on both the cultural and natural history of the area. I found the literature on the Joshua trees themselves — many of them 700 to 800 years old — and the large variety of birds to be found in the monument especially interesting. A self-guided nature trail at the center winds down through a pleasant palm oasis that was once home to Indians and some of the early white settlers in this area.

For those who prefer, there is a southern entrance to the monument just off I-10, at the town of Cottonwood Spring. If you opt for this route, you'll miss the various antique and souvenir shops scattered along the northern route. It's your loss.

Hidden Valley

Once inside the national monument, your first stop might well be Hidden Valley, an area of massive boulders and impressive rock formations that reportedly was once a hideout for cattle rustlers and other assorted

Rocky Trail.
Paths and trails in Joshua Tree National Monument are often rugged and rocky, but a visit to the little-traveled desert backcountry is worth the challenge.

Seal Rocks.
Carved by eons of wind and sand, Seal Rocks are an incongruous element in a forbidding land where the nearest ocean beach is hundreds of miles away.

Doug Emerson

outlaws of the Old West. Today, there is a campground tucked in among these massive formations, which are now popular with rock climbers. There are also a couple of trails here that provide a scenic route through the valley.

Salton View

If you take the paved road that winds south out of Hidden Valley it climbs eventually to a vista point called Salton View. At an elevation of 5,185 feet, this spot will give you a panoramic view of the desert floor all the way to the Mexican border. You'll also see the Salton Sea (235 feet below sea level), and the San Jacinto and San Gorgonio mountain ranges.

The Lost Horse Mine Trail

Backtracking from Salton View, take the narrow dirt side road that leads down to the trailhead for the Lost Horse Mine. The two-mile trail leads to the mine through a variety of desert flora. At the mine there are some well-preserved remnants of the industry that flourished here in the late 1800s. **Note:** It takes a good deal of time to walk to and from the mine, so don't take this trail if you are planning to spend only a few hours in the monument.

Lost Horse Mine.
Remnants of gold prospecting await the hardy hikers who take the time to walk the two-mile trail that leads here.

Steve Smith

If you want to take a leisurely tour of the region and remain in the comfort of your rig, I suggest you follow the self-guided Geology Falls Road motor trail that winds eighteen miles through some of the historic and scenic sights within the monument. Besides spectacular views of the surrounding area, this route leads to interesting exhibits on the Indians who lived here long before the arrival of the first gold prospectors in 1865.

National Park Service

Keys Ranch.
Also known as the Desert Queen, this ranch complex contains various structures and an odd assortment of cars, trucks, and farming equipment acquired by desert rat William Keys.

The Desert Queen (Keys) Ranch

Of course, no visit to Joshua Tree National Monument is complete without a stop at the Desert Queen Ranch (also known as Keys Ranch). This ranch was originally the homestead of William Keys, a colorful desert rat who settled here just after World War I and remained until his death in 1969. Within the ranch complex stands a well-preserved cluster of structures that includes the Keys's farmhouse, guest cabins, and a schoolhouse. A small family cemetery also lies within the compound, each tombstone carved personally by Keys. The ranch may be viewed only by means of a guided tour conducted by rangers from mid-February through Memorial Day and from mid-October through mid-December. A schedule of the tours is posted at the visitor center in Twentynine Palms.

The Palm Springs Area

For a sharp contrast to the rugged, barren beauty of Joshua Tree National Monument, I suggest you take some time to stop and explore the streets and byways of nearby Palm Springs, Rancho Mirage, and Palm Desert. Although these desert communities have a reputation of being the watering holes of the wealthy and powerful, you might be surprised to learn they are also hospitable stopoffs for RVers. Besides finding some excellent RV resorts here, superb restaurants, unique shopping opportunities, and some of the finest golf courses in the nation are available. A few words of warning: The Palm Springs area is overrun each year by thousands of college students who have made their pilgrimage here an annual spring-break event. Unless you're an enthusiast of rock music played at deafening levels, traffic jams, and general mayhem, avoid this place like the plague during Easter week.

Malevolent Presence.
Seemingly sculpted by some dark force, Skull Rock overlooks the desert landscape with an eerie countenance.

George Ostertag

A Date with the Absurd.
Camel races are a hilarious highlight of the annual National Date Festival in Indio, which celebrates the yearly harvest of some 6,000 tons of (you guessed it) dates.

Riverside County's National Date Festival

Indio's Date Festival

One celebration I recommend you don't miss, however, is the National Date Festival held annually in February in the tiny desert town of Indio. This event is said to draw nearly a quarter of million visitors each year from all over the world. They come here to help the local date growers celebrate their annual harvest of some 6,000 tons of dates.

Within a region of just over 5,000 acres — the only date-producing area in the U. S. — the farmers here grow, harvest, and package more than thirty varieties of high-quality dates. During the festival you can find creamed and chopped dates, as well as colorful gift packages of date chunks, date paste, date crystals, date balls, date butter, date pies, date cookies, and an assortment of date pastries and cakes. Most notable perhaps is the date shake that was invented by Russell Charles Nicoll, an early resident of Indio, who first offered this cool concoction to road-weary desert travelers some fifty years ago.

Other Desert Destinations

Having eaten your fill of dates and participated in at least a few of the festivities, the next move is up to you. From Indio you can follow the hordes of motorists making the dash across the desert to Las Vegas, or you can strike out for the unknown. To the south there is the Salton Sea (plenty of campgrounds) and the vast Imperial Valley. If you're feeling a little more adventurous, try heading out on some of those desert backroads that lie north of I-10 and east of Joshua Tree National Monument. You may be surprised at what you find.

POINTS OF INTEREST: California Tour 8

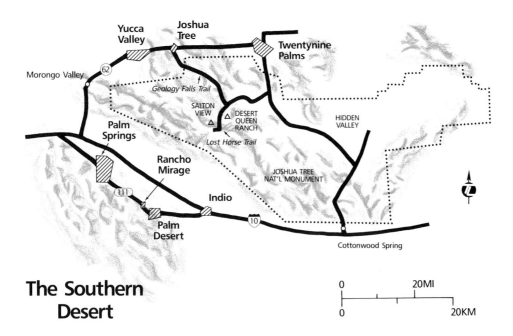

The Southern Desert

0   20MI

0   20KM

ACCESS: *I-15* east of Barstow, south by various routes; *I-10,* north on *SR 62* to Twentynine Palms.

INFORMATION: *Indio Chamber of Commerce,* P.O. Box TTT, Indio, California 92202, (619) 347-0676; *Joshua Tree National Monument,* 74485 National Monument Drive, Twentynine Palms, California 92278; *Palm Springs Chamber of Commerce,* 190 West Amado, Palm Springs, California 92262, (619) 325-1577.

ANNUAL EVENTS:
Indio: *National Date Festival,* Feb.

Palm Springs: *Gordon Bennett Balloon Race,* April; *Palm Springs Vintage Grand Prix,* November.

MUSEUMS AND GALLERIES:
Indio: *Coachella Valley Museum and Cultural Center,* 82-616 Miles Avenue, Tuesday–Sunday, year-round, (619) 342-6651.

Palm Springs: *Palm Springs Desert Museum,* 101 Museum Drive, Tuesday–Sunday, late September to May, closed major holidays, (619) 325-7186.

SPECIAL ATTRACTIONS:
Palm Springs: *Palm Springs Aerial Tramway,* Tramway Road, three miles southwest of SR 111, daily year-round, except first week in August. Affords spectacular views of desert and San Jacinto Mountain range; also provides access to mountain trails, (619) 325-1391.

RESTAURANTS: There are a number of fine restaurants in Palm Springs and the surrounding resort area. Check locally for listings.

National Park Service

Doug Emerson

Index

Page numbers in **boldface** refer to illustrations in the text.